TWENTIETH CENTURY VIEWS

The aim of this series is to present the best in contemporary critical opinion on major authors, providing a twentieth century perspective on their changing status in an era of profound revaluation.

Maynard Mack, *Series Editor*
Yale University

MODERN
BRITISH
DRAMATISTS

NEW PERSPECTIVES

Edited by
John Russell Brown

Prentice-Hall, Inc. A SPECTRUM BOOK *Englewood Cliffs, N.J.*

Library of Congress Cataloging in Publication Data

Modern British dramatists, new perspectives.

(Twentieth century views)
"A Spectrum Book."
Bibliography: p.
Includes index.
1. English drama—20th century—History and criticism—
Addresses, essays, lectures.   I. Brown, John Russell.
II. Series.
PR737.M58   1984   822'.91'09   83-21261
ISBN 0-13-588021-1
ISBN 0-13-588013-0 (pbk.)

Editorial/production supervision by William P. O'Hearn
Wood engraving © 1984 by Vivian J. Berger
Manufacturing buyer: Edward J. Ellis

10 9 8 7 6 5 4 3 2 1

ISBN 0-13-588021-1

ISBN 0-13-588013-0 {PBK.}

PRENTICE-HALL INTERNATIONAL, INC. *(London)*
PRENTICE-HALL OF AUSTRALIA PTY. LIMITED, *(Sydney)*
PRENTICE-HALL CANADA INC. *(Toronto)*
PRENTICE-HALL OF INDIA PRIVATE LIMITED *(New Delhi)*
PRENTICE-HALL OF JAPAN, INC. *(Tokyo)*
PRENTICE-HALL OF SOUTHEAST ASIA PTE. LTD. *(Singapore)*
WHITEHALL BOOKS LIMITED *(Wellington, New Zealand)*
EDITORA PRENTICE-HALL DO BRASIL LTDA. *(Rio de Janeiro)*

Contents

Acknowledgments

Quotations from contemporary British plays are made by the kind permission of the following:

John Arden's *The Waters of Babylon,* copyright © 1961 by John Arden; *Live Like Pigs,* copyright © 1962 by John Arden; and *The Workhouse Donkey,* copyright © 1964 by John Arden, by permission of the publishers, Methuen, London, and the Grove Press, Inc., New York; John Arden's *The Bagman,* by permission of the publishers, Methuen, London, and of Margaret Ramsay, 14a Goodwin's Court, London; and John Arden's *Non-Stop Connolly Show* by permission of the publishers, Pluto Press, London.

Alan Ayckbourn's *Absent Friends, Absurd Person Singular, Bedroom Farce,* and *Norman Conquests* by permission of Chatto & Windus Ltd., London, and Grove Press, Inc., New York; Alan Ayckbourn's *Confusions* and *Relatively Speaking* by permission of Margaret Ramsay Ltd.

Edward Bond's *Saved* and *Lear* by permission of the publishers, Methuen, London.

Peter Nichols's *Passion Play* by permission of the publishers, Methuen, London.

Joe Orton's *Funeral Games, Loot,* and *What the Butler Saw* by permission of the publishers, Methuen, London.

John Osborne's *Look Back in Anger* and *The Entertainer* by permission of the publishers, Faber & Faber, London, and S. G. Phillips Inc. (Criterion Books), New York.

Harold Pinter's *The Birthday Party* and *The Homecoming* by permission of the publishers, Methuen, London.

Tom Stoppard's *Rosencrantz and Guildenstern Are Dead, After Magritte, Jumpers, Artist Descending a Staircase, Travesties,* and *Dirty Linen* by permission of the publishers, Faber & Faber, London, and Grove Press, Inc., New York.

David Storey's *Life Class* and *Home* (Penguin Books Ltd.) by permission of A. M. Heath & Company Ltd.

Introduction

by John Russell Brown

For ten years and more after the end of the Second World War, British theatre lived quietly. With little argument and no fuss, its scattered forces were reassembled and work was put in hand to restore the production lines that had been in action before hostilities began. Some few oddities were accommodated, like a "revival" of verse drama—but that innovation did not challenge old theatrical forms or literary felicities—and translations or adaptations of plays by Lorca, Giradoux, and Anouilh. Reports from abroad that praised the "epic" theatre of Bertolt Brecht, the "holy" theatre of Antonin Artaud, or the "absurd" theatre of Ionesco did not dint the self-absorption of those who were busy restaging Shakespeare, Chekov, Ibsen, Shaw, and Restoration comedy. Most directors, actors, and authors were content to maintain a much narrower theatrical tradition, without brand names or manifestos. The best products of this theatre were well-managed reproductions of desirable or deeply felt life as it might be lived in small groups of attractive people in exceptional circumstances.

Bold and passionate plays were being written in English at this time, but their authors were all American—Arthur Miller, Tennessee Williams, and Eugene O'Neill. These works did get staged in London, but they were received like rare trophies from another world or like survivals from an earlier turmoil that had been represented already in the prewar plays of O'Casey and Synge. As the new European dramatists went largely unperformed and unconsidered, so no one seems to have thought of imitating these trans-Atlantic authors, still less of founding a new kind of British drama.

At its best the rehabilitated theatre was intriguing, temperamental and, less frequently, thoughtful. But by common consent, all its business was carried on without noise or passion, as if a prolonged convalescence had to take its agreeable course in order to ensure full recovery from the shock and rigours of war. Seldom were present-day issues posed on the stage, and few signs could be seen in the theatre of the far-reaching and totally unprecedented changes that were taking place in thought, feeling, and society throughout the world.

This composure was first shaken by Samuel Beckett's *Waiting for Godot*. This had been produced in Paris in the original French in 1953 and came to London in a translation by its author in 1955. It soon transferred from the pocket-sized Arts Theatre to the Criterion and was produced subsequently throughout the world. The impasse had been broken and innovation became recognized as not only possible but, more important than that, necessary. If British drama was going to have any life at all in the 1950s and beyond, it would have to catch up with its audience and with the other arts.

Beckett, an ex-patriate Irishman who had started publishing novels, poems, and criticism before the war, continued to write mostly in French. He lived in Paris and made only short and infrequent visits to London. But within five years many new dramatists had had their first works produced in Britain and were more or less established in a theatre that wanted, now, to surprise, challenge, and enlighten its audience, as well as continuing to entertain it: Some writers sought to transform their audience or to seek a new one.

Within ten years, John Osborne, Harold Pinter, and Arnold Wesker had all had successes in the West End of London and, together with John Arden, were engaged on productive and individually innovative careers. Dozens of other new writers had committed themselves to the theatre and were creating plays that could not have been dreamed of only a few years earlier.

The long delay before British theatre emerged from the restrictions of the postwar years may account for the vigor and confidence of the new growth when, at last, that did appear. Instead of being suspicious of old skills and rejecting them out of hand, the innovators put them to good use for their own purposes. Harold Pinter and John Osborne had worked as actors in the early 1950s, learning how to perform in the works of Shakespeare, Coward, Wilde, Shaw, and other classics, and finding much in them to enjoy. Pinter had been a member of two classical repertory companies, run by Anew McMaster and by Sir Donald Wolfit, actor–managers in the nineteenth-century tradition. John Arden developed his own stagecraft alongside an active study of English medieval drama, popular ballads, and the plays of Aristophanes and Ben Jonson: he was also influenced by the stand-up comics of the music hall that had flourished in Britain at the turn of the previous century. When these writers became aware of European innovations—Brecht's Berlinner Ensemble visited London in 1956 and Ionesco's shorter plays became popular in English during the late 1950s—they were not tempted into slavish imitation; they had their own strengths on which to build.

At very much the same time, Joan Littlewood moved her Theatre Workshop Company from Manchester to the East End of London and so provided a distinctively British kind of director's theatre to challenge the production techniques of three or four previous decades. She trained a group of actors in the style of British Music Hall and of the *commedia dell'Arte* of the Italian renaissance. She also employed the dialectical and research methods of Brecht and produced plays that had been especially written or developed during group rehearsals. British and European classics were staged in productions that lacked the glamour and historicity for which other directors were still striving but put in their place Joan Littlewood's own notions of contemporary relevance and innovative interpretation. During the late 1950s this company moved some of its productions to the West End and set high standards for vitality, clarity of purpose, and popularity. It was a robust and essentially comic theatre that tackled major themes in an immediately enjoyable style.

Such were the beginnings of modern British drama, and an earlier Spectrum anthology of criticism, published in 1968, provided an appraisal of the first ten years of growth. At that

time its staying power was still in question: The sudden outburst of creativity might have been short-lived, without development or repetition. But the emphasis that I have given here
to its slow beginnings and the dramatists' awareness of ancient
traditions are two possible reasons for the continuous adaptation and reserves of energy that have characterized the following years and now demand a much fuller and broader appraisal of the work of modern British dramatists since the
mid-1950s.

By 1980, Osborne, Arden, and Wesker had proved their
resourcefulness and also their independence. None of these
three leaders was to hold center stage for long, but each
continued to write for the theatre and to seek the appropriate
conditions for the performance of his plays. After a number
of disappointments and protests, John Arden came to despise
professional and established theatre; his later practice has
been to set up his own production companies, for specific
audiences and occasions, and often using amateur actors.
Osborne and Wesker have had to wait a long time before
getting the casts and directors that offered good chances for
some of their later works. In the process they have both
become independent of fashion: Wesker has often been his
own director, especially in productions outside Britain, and
Osborne has given his plays to whichever company could best
support the skilled actors who are attracted by his passionate
and eloquent dialogue, even while his plays have become
more discursive or more bitterly satirical.

Harold Pinter is the only one of the original innovators
who has continued to hold the attention of critics and audiences without being forced onto the defensive or the side
lines. But he has extended the range of his engagement by
working as a director of other people's plays and as a writer of
film scripts. Such diversification followed naturally from his
earlier experience as actor and writer of radio and television
plays, and it has influenced his theatre writing in many ways,
technically and, most importantly, in keeping it open to new
themes and new perceptions. Since the mid-1960s, Pinter's
output for the theatre has been small, with full-length plays
appearing once every five years or so, but his target has kept

moving ahead into new territories, and his weaponry is always being both refined and extended. Nothing is easy, one feels, for this dramatist, but the possibilities within which he works are always changing. He knows his craft thoroughly and passes beyond its apparent limitations. For all the precision of his dialogue and stage directions, his work has freedom, lightness, and adventure.

Alongside these four dramatists, many others started to write extensively for the theatre, and each year that has passed others have joined them. By the end of the 1970s, in the judgment of many observers, drama had become the dominant literary form in Britain. More plays are being written than ever before, by a greater number of authors and in a wider range of styles.

Some influences from Europe have been absorbed. The vogue for Ionesco lasted only a few years, and Artaud's theory and practice, while more pervasive and enduring, have contributed to small companies working on adaptations of classical texts or documentary material rather than to the development of individual dramatists. But productions of Brecht and, latterly, of Büchner, Wedekind, Horvarth, and other German-language dramatists, have shown writers new techniques of staging and character presentation. The Royal Shakespeare, the Royal Court, and the National Theatre companies have all staged Brecht in the 1960s and 1970s, sometimes translated by young radical dramatists such as Howard Brenton and Steve Gooch, and most regional theatres have followed their lead. These productions have given living proof to writers that theatre can tackle larger issues than those familiar in the personal or intense dramas of the 1940s, 1950s, and early 1960s. They have also pointed to a more thoughtful and less conventional comedy. New British dramatists have moved toward public themes, even though a truly popular audience and a fully achieved epic theatre have not been established anywhere in Britain. John Osborne, John Arden, Edward Bond, Christopher Hampton, David Hare, David Edgar, Howard Brenton, Howard Barker, and Steve Gooch are among those most clearly influenced by radical German theatre.

Other influences have been Shakespeare's plays and
Jacobean tragedies and comedies. Shakespeare's histories in
Royal Shakespeare Company productions, culminating in
1964 with the consecutive staging of all the Henry IV, V, and
VI plays, and productions by Bill Gaskill of Middleton and by
Trevor Nunn of Tourneur's *Revenger's Tragedy* were ac-
claimed on all sides and have had a sustained influence. Edward Bond has prepared his own version of Webster's *White
Devil* (1612) and based a play of his own on Shakespeare's *King
Lear*. Brenton has adapted *Measure for Measure* to a modern
setting and based his *Thirteenth Night* (1981) on *Julius Caesar*
and *Macbeth*. In their own independent work, these writers
and many others have imitated the sharp, imagistic, and passionate writing of the Jacobeans (very different from the
spare, deliberate objectivity of Brecht), their direct address to
the audience, varied and violent action, and conflicts of style
between high and low, pathetic and ribald, bawdy and ceremonial. Peter Barnes's *Ruling Class* (1968), Charles Wood's
Veterans (1972), David Hare's *Knuckle* (1974), Stephen
Poliakoff's *City Sugar* (1975), and Howard Barker's *That Good
between Us* (1977), together with the high-charged comedy of
Joe Orton's *What the Butler Saw* (1969), are all dependent to
some degree on the vibrancy of Elizabethan and Jacobean
drama as it was produced in Britain by the same companies
that staged the work of the newest generation of playwrights.

Pulling in another direction, the speed, intimacy, and
verrisimilitude of film and television have also conditioned
new writing for the theatre. The action of many recent plays
cuts quickly from a public to private setting, from a wide to
narrow focus, and back again. Silences are held by movement
on stage that is specified meticulously in stage directions or by
changes of rhythm or action. Actual occupations from ordinary life are enacted with a high degree of verrisimilitude: In
Arnold Wesker's *Four Seasons* (1965) an apple streudel is made
on stage; in David Storey's *Changing Room* (1971) a rugby team
cleans up after a game; in David Rudkin's *Ashes* (1973) a young
husband and wife undergo medical examination for infer-
tility; in Robert Holman's *Rooting* (1979) a pig sty full of real

pigs is mucked out; and in Neil Dunn's *Steaming* (1981) girls enjoy a Turkish bath.

While television was establishing itself as a highly productive and widely popular entertainment, sophisticated technical equipment and production procedures were developed to serve its needs and these, in turn, have influenced the theatre. Lighting, for example, is controlled now by computer technology; projected images, remote-controlled scenic units, and multichannelled sound equipment have all become commonplace; and, most importantly perhaps, the director is today in almost unchallenged control of a theatre production, being the one person who is able to coordinate all its innumerable complications. New techniques are introduced wherever finances permit or innovation requires. They have transformed the business of staging plays before live audiences and, consequently, modified how dramatists conceive and write.

The physical and organizational conditions of the first performance of a stage play have become even more crucial elements in the successful launching of a new playwright. So much depends on what is called the "set up" that more and more established dramatists insist that their work be staged only by the directors they have come to trust over a period of years. Each new play by Harold Pinter is directed by Peter Hall; Peter Wood directs Tom Stoppard's; and Harold Pinter, Simon Gray's. Peter Shaffer gave a number of his to John Dexter and then, in 1979, *Amadeus* went to Peter Hall as director and John Bury as designer, both of whom had worked earlier on his *Battle of the Shrivings*. Even plays that can be staged very simply are presented more satisfactorily by a director and special group of actors who are known to the dramatist and respond fully to his ideas; so many options are now open in technique, style, and physical resources that a secure base for the production of a new play seems almost obligatory. Some writers have been associated very closely with particular producing companies: David Hare and Howard Brenton were involved with starting and running the Portable Theatre and then worked with the Royal Court

Theatre and the Nottingham Playhouse; Hare subsequently directed Brenton's *Weapons of Happiness* at the National Theatre in 1976 and has continued to direct all his own work. Edward Bond started by giving his plays to a group of directors associated with the Royal Court, but from the late 1970s onward has directed them himself for the National or the Court.

Alan Ayckbourn is the writer who most fully controls the production of his plays. He works on each new script for performance at the Stephen Joseph Theatre in Scarborough, Yorkshire, where he is both artistic director and chief executive. He schedules the plays himself, casts them, directs them, and is in charge of every element of their staging and financing. By the late 1970s, his control was extended still further, so that, having revised the scripts in the light of their first performances and their audiences' reactions in Scarborough, he now redirects them for their London premieres. In dialogue, individual characterization, theme, and action, Ayckbourn seems more traditional than many of his contemporaries, but his finesse in handling both the technical and the human elements of the production process means that his comedies are very finely judged and cunningly planned; they have the speed, shifting awareness, and nervousness of contemporary sensibility. Their characters seem caught in a world more complicated than they can understand; they reach for freedom, as they find themselves constricted by processes that both propel and confine them. Alan Ayckbourn is innovative because he uses in fullest measure the contrivance of theatrical production both to entertain and to share his fear of destruction.

Some attempts have been made to offset the growing power of the director who can quite as easily destroy as ensure a play's success and can restrict rather than release the performance of the actors. The most successful have been the Joint Stock Theatre productions. This company hired dramatists in the 1970s and early 1980s to work alongside actors, director, and designer in the development of new scripts for performance. Its method is for actors to agree on a theme and then, with author and director, to research, observe, improvise, and question. The final script evolves out of a common experience and is adjusted nicely and deeply to the qualities that each individual can bring to performance. Howard Brenton's *Epsom Downs* (1977), David Hare's *Fanshen* (1975), Barrie Keefe's adaptation of Middleton's *Mad World My Masters* (1976), and Stephen Lowe's *Ragged Trousered Philanthropist* (1978) are all products of this company's cooperative work and are texts that use actors boldly and resourcefully, needing only simple staging resources.

Other dramatists have worked on a single play over and over again, as it has been planned, researched, improvised, rehearsed, given a public reading, and then perhaps a "workshop" showing before it is finally prepared for a full-scale theatre production. Some plays have been given two or three productions under varying conditions, the text being modified for each occasion. Often a first production is in a very small theatre and the text elaborated at a later date for a "main house" production. David Edgar's *Destiny* (1976), David Rudkin's *Sons of Light* (1976), and Snoo Wilson's *Glad Hand* (1978) each progressed through several changes of staging, director, auditorium, and audience.

The profession of playwright in Britain in the 1980s offers little scope to an author who works in isolation and sends a complete manuscript to a theatre from some distant retreat. Besides being involved in the process of production, dramatists often have experience of television and film as well. They are paid to attend rehearsals in both subsidized and commercial theatres, and from the numerous previews that have replaced the "pre-London tryouts" and are accompanied by further rehearsals they are able to learn a great deal about theatre craft and the reactions of their audiences. It is a thriving profession for a writer who, besides the gifts of a strong imagination and an ability to use words and visual images, has also the will to engage with fellow artists of complementary and contrasting abilities. Perhaps this has brought into being a well-trodden path of fashionable effectiveness and has silenced some of the most individual voices, but modern British drama has held its own against the competition of the electronic media by using every possible means for in-

creasing the excitement and power of stage performance.
Many British dramatists are alive and well in the 1970s and
1980s, with the energy, subtlety, and resilience that is needed
for survival in their time; and their plays have become more
able to reflect the complications of modern awareness and
existence.

Any study of modern British drama must pay more attention to the conditions of performance than books concerned
with the drama of earlier periods. So this Spectrum anthology
contains some carefully judged theatre reviews, which give a
sense of particular performances; and all the contributors are
aware, in some degree, of the stage life of the plays.

But, as in other ages, it is still the dramatists who lead the
theatre's advance into new territories: The director is yet to
arrive who is able to alter singlehandedly the way in which
actors "hold the mirror up to nature." The effective innovators are dramatists, and it is upon them that this book
centers attention. The opening chapters are concerned with
three of those who broke the postwar impasse—John Osborne, Harold Pinter, and John Arden—judging them more
for their lasting contributions than for their initial successes,
as in the earlier Spectrum anthology. Then the main body of
the book considers those writers who have gained and held
attention through the 1960s and 1970s, and into the 1980s:
Alan Ayckbourn, Edward Bond, Peter Shaffer, Peter Nichols,
Tom Stoppard, and David Storey. The more interesting
younger   writers—Hare,   Brenton,   Hampton,   and
Poliakoff—and some who have written only a few stage
plays—such as Trevor Griffiths, David Edgar, and David
Rudkin—are also studied. From chapter to chapter a wider
view is established of the theatre itself, and so the work of
other writers can be placed and some general influences and
developments discerned. *Look Back in Anger* is used as a touchstone in many of the studies so that a perspective in time can be
provided.

The anthology opens with an account by Gareth Lloyd
Evans of the arrival of John Osborne and a reassessment of his
innovations and more traditional strengths. Harold Pinter is

Introduction 11

then the subject of two chapters, but because another Spectrum anthology, edited by Arthur Ganz (1972), considers the
earlier plays individually, I have printed here only my own
account of Pinter's dramaturgy, which tries to describe the
essential qualities of his writing for the stage, and Benedict
Nightingale's perceptive review of *Betrayal* in performance, a
play too recent to be included in Professor Ganz's anthology.

Julian Hilton's chapter next brings together three very
different dramatists, Christopher Hampton, David Storey,
and John Arden, born respectively in 1946, 1933, and 1930;
he shows how one particular theatre company, devoted to the
encouragement of new writing, has encouraged three very
different talents to fulfillment. But the individual nature of
most writers requires separate and distinctive appraisal, and
so each of the next seven chapters deals with one writer only.
Katharine Worth shows the traditional skills of Joe Orton as
well as his unique tone and conceptual energy. Hersh Zeifman
looks closely at Tom Stoppard's wordplay and from that tight
focus is able to reveal the wider implications of the plays and
their structural characteristics. Guido Almansi's account of
Alan Ayckbourn also looks comedy carefully in the face to
show recurring ideas behind the words and actions of the
plays that have both drawn large audiences and received
harsh and curt dismissal by critics who look for explicit meanings and evaluations in drama.

Peter Shaffer and David Hare are, in different ways,
writers who use highly charged situations and eloquent
characters. The plays of both must be studied in performance
if their power is to be realized, and so two reviews are reprinted here, by Walter Kerr and Colin Ludlow.

The plays of Edward Bond are strong in explicit argument, and there have been several studies of the themes and
ideas informing them. Some, like the books by Tony Coult
and by Malcolm Hays and Philip Roberts, limit themselves to
responding to the plays in their own terms, but Christopher
Innes's chapter in this anthology takes a more critical view: It
considers both the changing theatrical means and the changing meanings, and compares Bond with several of his contemporaries, especially some German dramatists.

June Schlueter's account of Peter Nichols's *Passion Play* is not a review of a performance, but a response to the text in the light of plays by Pinter, O'Neill, and Brian Friel that have used similar techniques of presentation to different effects, and a structural analysis that leads to a probing of what the play as a whole shows an audience about its characters.

The concluding chapter, by C. W. E. Bigsby, brings together a number of playwrights who have called for an unashamedly political theatre. Here Arnold Wesker is considered briefly as a leader in what has become the most articulate group of writers, all concerned to grapple with pressing social issues. In a way that would have been unthinkable in 1955, the critic discusses both British and European dramatists, both dramatists and sociologists, politicians and philosophers. It is a critical response to a theatre that is defined and limited by a thoroughly contemporary consciousness, even when that militates against the pronounced intentions of its dramatists.

John Osborne and Naturalism

by Gareth Lloyd Evans

Both Arnold Wesker and John Osborne have been hailed as exciting innovators in modern drama. Hindsight, which always has an opportunity to display a wisdom denied to contemporaries of an event, raises some doubts about both the extent and the nature of their innovations. Wesker, for example, now seems important less as the man who gave the working class the freedom of the stage, than for his use of the vernacular and for his contribution to the onset of anti-heroic drama.

Much larger claims were made for John Osborne after the admittedly sensational success of the first production of *Look Back in Anger* in 1956. The chief chronicler of the fifties and sixties, John Russell Taylor, is empyrean in his enthusiasm—for him Osborne "started everything off." Only slightly less ecstatic is his view that the play was the first "type-image of the new drama."

But Osborne has been worshipped—the word hardly seems inappropriate—for other reasons. His protagonist, Jimmy Porter, has been regarded as the first non-hero—an opinion which ignores Stanley Kowalski who, by the time *Look Back in Anger* was written was well known and had spawned, in films, a number of progeny of his own type. Again—and Taylor echoes this opinion—Osborne's Jimmy was said, and still is by some, to represent a postwar generation in his anger, petulance, dissatisfaction, infirmity of purpose, railing, com-

"John Osborne and Naturalism." From Gareth Lloyd Evans, *The Language of Modern Drama,* Everyman's University Library (London, Melbourne, and Toronto: J. M. Dent & Sons Ltd., 1977), pp. 102–13. Copyright © 1977 by Gareth Lloyd Evans. Reprinted by permission of the publisher.

plaining. All these descriptive words have been used by commentators to describe Jimmy Porter. Yet, which generation is this supposed to represent? Many of Jimmy's age at the time would not have recognized themselves in him. What, more and more, seems to be nearer the truth is that Jimmy is a mouthpiece for one man's disillusion about the society he lived in. John Osborne has been no slouch since 1956 in reiterating his views about society as he sees it—more and more in many of his public pronouncements he echoes, in an older way, a younger Porter.

And, of course, the play was hailed for the raw naturalism of its language. While allowing for the strong possibility that, at a time when censorship existed and, apparently, was exerted on the play, the language seemed permissive, there now seems room to doubt whether the word naturalism is apt, and even "raw" seems a relative word in the context of much of today's dramatic language.

The claims for Osborne's play have weakened, but the greatest blow was delivered by the author himself. He described it as a formal old-fashioned play. Osborne's candour is often mashed with what seems a mischievous compulsion to thicken the issue or stir contention, so that his own description must not be taken at face-value. In this case, however, a summary examination of the play reveals some interesting facts. It is a three-acter; it has a thoroughly conventional set; that is, in the old-fashioned sense, a box-set; the play has a very precise conventional pattern—statement, development, crisis and resolution—in dramatic and theatrical terms, even if, thematically, it is opaque and lacks direction; no special effects are required; the "situation" is naturalistic in that it could well be equated with real-life events. Indeed, a cursory examination alone amply confirms that Osborne's view of his play, is, indeed, forthright.

The two most persistent claims to innovation have been the vehemence and comprehensiveness of the protest and the nature of the language. They are closely connected and may therefore be examined as one. The first and perhaps the strongest impression of all that we receive in either reading or seeing the play is the rhythm that is set up between monologue and dialogue. Indeed, merely to hold the pages before your eyes and to turn them slowly reveals a visual pattern consisting of solid clumps of print (Jimmy's monologues) strung upon the thin wire of isolated lines (the dialogue). The dialogue, as such, which, of course, often involves Jimmy, too, is, on the whole, a neutral speech. Little attempt is made by Osborne to characterize through it, or to indicate class or accent. We have an occasional "girlie" and a "not 'arf" from Cliff the Welshman (to whom, unaccountably, "not 'arf" is confined), but otherwise, there is no identification, no individualization in this dialogue. For example, we may think here that this is yet another of Jimmy's self-indulgences—

> I was wrong, I was wrong! I don't want to be neutral, I don't want to be a saint. I want to be a lost cause, I want to be corrupt and futile!

—but we should be warned that it is, in truth, one of Alison's speeches! That is an example of an outburst, but the more moderate areas of dialogue reveal that we are very much in the domain of the "well-made play," a genre which so many of Osborne's admirers thought he was, by his scything newness, demolishing for ever. The "well-made" elements in the language have several aspects, and some of them are to be found in Jimmy's famous monologues, but the more obvious are in the dialogue.

The language of the "well-made" play always raises a question—"did people ever talk like this?" We do not ask the question of, say, Hamlet, or Mrs. Malaprop or Doolittle, not because their language is more "real," but because it convinces us in a way the "well-made" play is incapable of doing—it contains an illusion of actuality within the pattern of its design. The language of Shakespeare, Sheridan or Shaw creates, in relation to theme and plot, a truth of character: we are forced to believe, whereas with the well-made play part of the pleasure lies in the exercise of our disbelief.

There is a good deal of "well-made" dialogue in *Look Back in Anger*. Not only did no one ever talk like this—it creates with artificiality—but no characters firmly emerge out of it. The words remain as words, they often create nothing; they merely pass information:

> *Colonel.* Well, I'd better put this in the car then. We may as well get along. Your mother will be worried, I know. I promised her I'd ring her when I got here. She's not very well.
> *Helena.* I hope my telegram didn't upset her too much. Perhaps I shouldn't have—
> *Colonel.* Not at all. We were very grateful that you did. It was very kind of you, indeed. . . .

We must remind ourselves that the proof is in the hearing, however. The proof here is the extraordinary effect of a lack of dimension these two characters have on stage, even when performed by the most accomplished of players. It is not fulfilling the first requirement of dramatic language—the embodiment of individual character.

Yet another "well-made" feature of the language is evidenced by what may well be called by the actress playing the part the "sacrificial" dialogue given to Helena. It is sacrificial because it puts the actress in a posture where she has little chance of initiating any kind of action herself. She becomes a mere victim for the other person on stage who holds all the verbal weapons. In the final act, in the long scene between Alison and Helena, many of Helena's "speeches" consist of single sentences or phrases which either confirm something Alison has said or ask a question to enable Alison to proceed: "And it was true"; "I could hardly believe it myself"; "Maybe not. But I feel it just the same." The longer speeches, which these and other phrases interrupt, in which Helena tells of her feelings about Jimmy, are insufficient to quell the sense of a kind of dramatic futility in the part. Helena is only half-alive, and the Colonel is barely alive because like so many of their ilk in the well-made play their language is merely functional—and often barely that. Alison and Cliff give the illusion of being more rounded characters only because they have more to say and are involved much more in give-and-take with Jimmy. But their language, per se, is lacking in personality.

It is to Jimmy's language that we must look for evidence

of the raw naturalism which Osborne is said to have brought to the stage. It is naturalistic—that is, it has a degree of truth to actual spoken speech—but not in the sense in which the term is often applied today. That is, it is not naturalistic as so much contemporary dramatic speech is, using the lowest common denominator of the vernacular like Bond[1] for example, in *Saved*, or as so many television plays do. Jimmy's "naturalism" is special (to this extent he would probably be considered as élitist by a proponent of the most typical drama of the 1970s).

In the first place it is eloquent. It is not so much raw as vehement in a very lucid way. It sounds like the language of an educated man (and Jimmy, of course, is a university graduate) that has been carefully honed for stage purposes. It is, therefore, several stages higher in articulacy than the language employed by Wesker in the greater part of his Trilogy or by Shelagh Delaney in her celebrated *A Taste of Honey*—both dramatists associated by the commentators, for reasons that now seem illogical, with Osborne. The language of Jimmy is very similar to that of Dixon in Kingsley Amis's novel *Lucky Jim*. Indeed, Dixon's language is more "natural" to the group from which it derives than is Porter's. Osborne has amalgamated with the group-language a number of devices.

The group-language from which Jimmy's speech comes is undergraduate—not exclusively, but to a large extent, arts. It is a language which was and is acquired in the heady atmosphere of the favoured student pub, the common-room, the debating-society, the endless impromptu coffee-sessions in hall, house or digs. It is the language of educated youth feeling its feet and determined to put things right. It is the language of a certain conceit—often not a vicious or deep one, but a cosy one born of a self-awareness of intelligence, a sense of words, and a desire to chalk up a victory in the intellectual stakes.

It is, too, a language which many undergraduates never abandon. It is to be found, sometimes polished, sometimes

---

[1]See G. Lloyd Evans, *The Language of Modern Drama* (London: Dent, 1977), Chapter 11, for his discussion of Edward Bond.

sharpened, sometimes down-at-heel, sometimes sly, sometimes exactly the same, in parliament, in the law, in senior
common-rooms, in reunion dinners, in the occasional door-
to-door salesmen, in school staff rooms. Jimmy has it still in a
pristine form, but its content has been soured by time and
circumstance. It is a language that is catching—from time to
time Cliff gives evidences of having been infected by Jimmy,
but there is no doubt that his is a secondary version. He, as
Jimmy reminds us, is uneducated.

The characteristics of the language are eloquence, as we
have seen, frequent lucidity, a tendency to exaggeration
through repetition. It is, in a general analysis, always seeming
to be on the point of breaking into a public rhetorical speech:

> Reason and Progress, the old firm, is selling out! Everyone get out
> while the going's good. Those forgotten shares you had in the old
> traditions, the old beliefs are going up—up and up and up.

Because it is so aware of itself anything of depth which it
conveys seems to be created by accident. It cannot be trusted
to a consistency of logic or argument, though it can often
suddenly illuminate an idea or a feeling or an intuition:

> If you've no world of your own, it's rather pleasant to regret the
> passing of someone else's. I must be getting sentimental. But I
> must say it's pretty dreary living in the American Age—unless
> you're American of course.

Its most consistent quality is its drawing of attention to itself,
and it does this by a persistent attempt to be witty. It often is,
but the wit is always aggressive. It cannot be quiet because
quietness is an enemy to exhibition:

> All I know is that somebody's been sticking pins into *my* wax image
> for years. *(Suddenly)* Of course: Alison's mother! Every Friday, the
> wax arrives from Harrods, and all through the week-end she's
> stabbing away at it with a hatpin! Ruined her bridge game, I dare
> say.

But it can often be banal largely because it is always in danger
of losing a sense of fitness and proportion. When it is banal it is
then that a kind of youthful pathos can just be glimpsed
behind the cataract of words:

The heaviest, strongest creatures in this world seem to be the loneliest. Like the old bear, following his own breath in the dark forest. There's no warm pack, no herd to comfort him. The voice that cries out doesn't *have* to be a weakling's, does it?

To write of the language as if it were a dramatis persona may be objected to. The truth is, however, that in *Look Back in Anger* almost all that Jimmy is as character is derived from the personality of the language. The surface characteristics of this group-language added up give us the total of Jimmy Porter's temperament. To this extent, the language is protagonist. Except, that is, for two ingredients which Osborne has added.

The first is melodrama—that is, the use of language to appeal to the emotions in ways that are at best, obvious, at worst, crude. The "anger" of Jimmy Porter consists largely of a set of melodramatic forages into certain territories, an anger which seems less an emanation of some faith, principle or belief than a function of language. Jimmy is angry at so many things, but it is impossible to find any real source for the generation of the anger. He shouts in different sharps and flats, but we don't know why. All we can be sure of is his ability to appeal to emotions.

In the context an interesting observation was provided by a young company of players of very high professional capability, which was far too young to have recalled the sensational effect of the play in 1956, when recently having a first reading prior to production. None had read it before. The reaction was, for an older auditor, quite unexpected. The actors did not find naturalism, rawness, social significance, anger; instead they found old-fashioned melodrama. The actor playing Jimmy inquired what accent he was to use for (as he put it) "the different characters this chap pretends to be—most of them unconsciously funny."

The other ingredient is sentimentality. Again this emerges less as an inevitable facet of character than as a function of language. Rhetoric is often the mother of sentimental expression, with its recourse to repetition, its self-regarding rhythms, its tendency to seem impersonal while pushing unerringly towards the emotionally subjective. Jimmy Porter's character has a huge sentimental element within it—and, inevitably, we find that we can attribute it clearly to no specific experience he has had, or principle, or prejudice. It emerges through the rhetoric of his speech and we can only come to the conclusion that he does not so much feel it as luxuriate in the indulgence of listening to himself expressing it. No part of Jimmy's anger, hate, love, sentimentality is explicable except in terms of self-indulgence. And even that is a shallow fickle thing that is dependent upon the waywardness and versatility of his ability to talk himself into one posture or another. There is no surer evidence of this than in the famous speech about his dying father, hailed by many as an example of an underlying sensitivity and vulnerability in the angry, deprived, perturbed spirit of Jimmy Porter. In truth, what is remarkable about the speech is not any revelation of the deeper soul of Porter, but of the utter shallowness of his responses. The language as it grows more rhetorical, "turns on" the sentimentality, and as this proceeds, the object of the speech turns away from the dying father to Jimmy himself. He has talked himself into being a victim. His father was the stalking-horse for Jimmy's self-indulgent eloquence.

It would not by any means be generally agreed that [Osborne's] *The Entertainer* [1957] is a better and likely to be a more memorable play than *Look Back in Anger*. Perhaps a consensus of opinion would reveal the belief that its success was due to Laurence Olivier's performance as Archie Rice.

If a greater flexibility and variety in the use of language is a criterion of quality then the general view has to be questioned. *The Entertainer* seems to employ language in a richer dramatic way than its more illustrious forerunner—though it may well have pre-dated it, at least in a preliminary form of conception. Certainly there are strong echoes of Jimmy in it particularly in some of Archie's more rhetorical monologues; and over the whole there is Osborne's characteristic eloquence and sheer cleverness of phrasing. But the group-speech which is so strong an informing element in *Look Back in Anger* is firmly kept in place. It has to give room to very much more dramatically and theatrically rich speech; it does not have the chance to persuade us, as it does in the other play, that we are listening less to a dramatic embodiment of ideas and characters than a subjective cri-du-coeur, half in love with listening to its own expressions of itself.

The measure of its superiority as a true dramatic piece is the comparative richness of characterization. Two of the secondary characters—Archie's wife and his father—have a far more credible presence than any secondary character in *Look Back in Anger*. Phoebe (the wife) takes life through her accent which is implicit in her language:

> Blimey, you should know better than to ask me that! You know what a rotten memory I've got. Well, cheerio! *(She drinks)* Oooh, that's a nice drop of gin—some of the muck they give you nowadays—tastes like cheap scent. . . .

Phoebe's language is clipped, always on the edge of being formless, inconsequential. It has none of the listless functionalism of Helen, or the artiness of Cliff. Through what she says and the form in which she says it we know her.

The same is true of Billy (Archie's father). His innate kindness, his frayed but brave dignity, comes out of a kind of hesitancy of speech. He moves from phrase to phrase, not with the possibility of lurching into incomprehensibility like Phoebe, but with a bemused care for saying the right thing. Therefore, he turns from one theme to another, carefully, nervously, watchfully, and with a touch of grace:

> *Billy.* Oh, this is nice of you. Thank you. Still, if she stays in she only gets irritable. And I can't stand rows. Not any more. *(He stares in front of him)* No use arguing with Phoebe anyway. Would you like some beer? *(She shakes her head)* She just won't listen to you. Are you sure you won't?

Olivier or not, Archie Rice is a more explicable, credibly dynamic, affecting character than Jimmy Porter. His failure as a human being is an inability not so much to distinguish (as some critics have suggested) between illusion and reality, as to keep them apart. It has a piercing human relevance. The way in which the little world he dominates partakes of his own weakness is both poignant and bitter. And the particular nature of his failure is superbly embodied in his very employment—as a professional Fool.

The language of Archie Rice is formed in a mould similar to that used for the creation of Shakespeare's Fools. There is no evidence that Osborne was or is conscious of this, nor that he would accept the connection. Yet, he, like Shakespeare, realized that a special language is needed to express a character whose very function—as professional entertainer—forces him to live constantly on the boundary that separates illusion and reality, fiction and truth.

Like Touchstone, Feste and Lear's Fool, Archie expresses himself in a language which is really in a state of flux between commenting upon reality and creating a fiction. All four characters have a good deal of motley on their tongues, but there are moments when they "wear not motley in their brain."

Sometimes, like the Fools, Archie bursts into a song and prefaces or follows it with tart comment; sometimes he wraps up meaning in an anecdote which does not always easily make its point; often, like the Fools, he is berated for flippancy or coarseness, and often, like them, he appears to talk in the wild hope of getting applause. But, always, the flux between his function as entertainer and his status as human being and the irony between the language of illusion and reality is at work.

In Act I, Scene iv of *King Lear,* the Fool, operating within the same flux, tries to convince Lear of the stupidity of his division of the kingdom. He does it with an anecdote which, typically, is a play upon words:

Fool. Nuncle, give me an egg, and I'll give thee two crowns.
Lear. What two crowns shall they be?
Fool. Why, after I have cut the egg i' the middle and eat up the meat, the two crowns of the egg. When thou clovest they crown i' the middle, and gav'st away both parts, thou bor'st thine ass on thy back.

In Scene viii of *The Entertainer,* Archie Rice mocks the pretensions of politics. It is no less self-consciously contrived than that of Lear's Fool; it is no less efficient in its punning; it is no less received with intimidation. Above all, it is of the same order of expression, coming from the same kind of dramatic agent. Archie and the Fools would understand each other perfectly:

> *Archie.* There was a chap at my school who managed to get himself into the Labour Government, and they always said he was left of centre. Then he went into the House of Lords, and they made him an honourable fishmonger. Well, that just about wraps up the left of centre, doesn't it?
>
> *Frank.* You know, you don't know what you're talking about. . . .
>
> *Archie.* If you can dodge all the clichés dropping like bats from the ceiling, you might pick up something from me.

In more measured terms, this is what Lear's Fool is saying to Lear.

The close association of the language and character of Archie with the Fools is most poignantly realized in the relationship of songs to dialogue and to situation and, especially, in the end. The essential loneliness of the figure who always patrols the thin line between illusion and reality, truth and fiction, is as true of Rice as it is of Feste with his wind and the rain or Lear's Fool who goes to bed at noon. And, to complete their consanguinity, inside the loneliness of all of them, is the wry paradox—who is performer and who is audience? What is real and what is not? Who is Fool and who is wise man?

> Why should I care,
> Why should I let it touch me,
> Why shouldn't I?—
> *(He stops, the music goes on, as he walks over to Phoebe, who helps him on with his coat, and gives him his hat. He hesitates, comes back down to the floats)* You've been a good audience. Very good. A very *good* audience. Let me know where you're working tomorrow night— and I'll come and see you.

In *The Entertainer* Osborne handled language with a creative sensitivity he never again equalled except intermittently in *Inadmissible Evidence.* The nature of this creativity is an ability to endow character with language appropriate to it. The enemy to this is to allow language to be the slave of theme or attitude and, hence, to be the mouthpiece of the author. Osborne's strength as a dramatist lies first in the unremitting passion of his language enabling him to provide actors capable of taking it with the opportunity to produce memorable oratorical performances. He has, too, an immense virtuosity of theme and plot and a vigorously aggressive relationship to the follies of his times which, at best, is refreshing, at worst, excusable.

In *The Hotel in Amsterdam,* the character Laurie cries, "I work my drawers off and get written off twice a year as not fulfilling my early promise by some Philistine squirt drumming up copy." Twelve years elapsed between *Look Back in Anger* and that remark, but it sounds like Jimmy Porter—or Osborne. The early promise is constantly being fulfilled—but never overtaken.

Action and Control: *The Homecoming* and Other Plays by Harold Pinter

by John Russell Brown

Harold Pinter has explored words and gestures so consciously and meticulously that he may seem more interested in theatre language than in theatre speech. He treats the money in his pocket with extraordinary care, but is never seen to purchase anything with it. He *seems* to be like the vintage car enthusiast who keeps his vehicle in a garage, in perfect working order, and never uses it for going on a journey—only his car is constructed from up-to-the-minute materials, and he is always making new parts, or rather, new cars.

Such views of Pinter's finesse gather strength because nowhere do his plays contain argument about the nature of life, nor do they give explicit expression to policies or prophecies. On reflection, his scepticism about words is sufficient cause for this, but it is disconcerting to have nothing to quote in order to illustrate an author's engagement with the world he lives in. Moreover, the basic elements of drama, the normal structural foundations, seem inconsiderable in his plays. The plots are slight, and can be told in few words. The characters do not explain where they have come from, or the causes of their attitudes and actions. Social and political background is sketched only by passing remarks, hints and ambiguities. There seems little substance in either narrative or theme, or social portraiture.

Pinter, himself, has encouraged us to suppose that he

writes without any palpable purpose: "What I write has no
obligation to anything other than to itself," he once said.[1] He
has never contrived a play as vehicle or embodiment for "any
kind of abstract idea," and "I wouldn't know a symbol if I saw
one," he has asserted.[2] He will not pose as reformer or social
commentator:

> If I were to state any moral precept it might be: Beware of the
> writer who puts forward his concern for you to embrace, who
> leaves you in no doubt as to his worthiness, his usefulness, his
> altruism, who declares that his heart is in the right place, and
> ensures that it can be seen, in full view, a pulsating mass where
> his characters ought to be. What is presented so much of the
> time, as a body of active and positive thought, is in fact a body
> lost in a prison of empty definition and cliché.[3]

But in all this, there is an obvious seriousness that reaches
beyond the mechanics of theatre or indulgent self-
gratification. When Robert Bolt wrote an article attacking his
fellow-dramatists for lack of purpose and staying power,
Pinter questioned his basic criteria. Bolt had dismissed
Ionesco in one sentence:

> Ionesco seems to me to be very private, rather sexual, and
> obscure, and therefore fundamentally rather frivolous.

"Why?" rejoined Pinter:

> Private, sexual, obscure, *therefore* frivolous. Even if one were to
> agree with the postulates, I see nothing axiomatic about the
> conclusion.[4]

In effect, Pinter has questioned, seriously and continuously,
the traditional subject matter and traditional purposes of
drama. His meticulous techniques of language and gesture
serve a consistent and active dramatic purpose. He dispenses
with verbal statement, because he distrusts it; he follows no
recognized rules of dramatic structure unless he needs to do

---

[1]"Between the Lines," *The Sunday Times* (London), 4 March 1962.
[2]"Writing for Myself," *Twentieth Century*, Vol. CLXIX (1961), 1008,
p. 174.
[3]"Between the Lines," op. cit.
[4]"Between the Lines," op. cit.

so. He hides his hand (and his heart) in order to win at the game in which he finds himself involved.

While, like Keats, Pinter rejects writers "with a palpable design upon us," he still, again like Keats, seeks "truth" in the whole as in the detail of his work. It is this overall control, expressed in the relationships between the smallest details, that most clearly shows the seriousness and, indeed, the utility of his plays.

His general strategy is progressive discovery, and in our examinations of individual words and gestures this mastering plan has already been observed at work. The warfare under smokescreens of speech, the manoeuvres for domination implicit in entries and exits, each partial statement of a character's engagement in the dramatic situation, all lead forward from activity to clarification, from effort to understanding. The conclusion is often marked by violence, a kind of explosion necessary to realign the forces of human mass and movement. Elsewhere, the end brings some quiet recognition of a shift of power that had been working surreptitiously throughout the action, or some new contact between characters or, more frequently, some gesture indicating their necessary isolation.

Nearly always in Pinter's plays, the action seems at the last moment to be held up, arrested: the dramatic situation now becomes static, as if energies have reached a point of balance or exhaustion. Each play, as it is performed, has a moment-by-moment excitement in that, for characters and audience alike, awareness is almost wholly in the active present—talk of past or future is from the point of view of the present moment—but, at the conclusion of each play, time seems to stop: all intimations of what has been or might be, seem now to be satisfied or effectively kept at bay; no one has another step to take. It is not unlike a stalemate at chess, for the final impasse has become progressively necessary through the elimination of other possibilities of manoeuvre; and, when it is at last declared, the minds of the audience are able to "see" the preceding action, reflected in that static confrontation.

Because Pinter works on his plays as if they were explorations of the potential energies within a small number of characters, he requires almost no story-line. Their action needs, rather, variation and fluidity by means of which the characters can encounter a wide set of stimulants and possibilities. In early plays, like *The Room* or *The Birthday Party,* entries and exits were used to shift the balance of power within a small narrative development. By means of visits and departures, and the ordinary routines of living, together with the theatrical devices of prolonged silence, sustained utterance or exploitation of ignorance, Pinter was able to change the effectiveness of individual characters, and bring a full range of reactions into play. By the time he wrote *The Caretaker,* he was ready to use black-outs (and fade-outs) within an Act to suggest a change of time and so permit instantaneous realignment; and this is developed in *The Lover* and *The Collection,* both first shown on television where this device is a standard means of providing the necessary variety of visual image and speed of exposition. *The Dwarfs* has the greatest fluidity of all, with little reference to a continuous story-line and no continuous sense of time; it moves from situation to situation, and from one theatrical style to another, according to the need to clarify what happens within the mind of Len, the central character. The coherence of this play depends almost wholly on the audience being able to follow Len's shifts of consciousness, his subterfuges and attacks, as they become necessary to him, not as he responds to a sequence of recognizable day-by-day occurrences.

For two television plays, *Night School* (1960) and *A Night Out* (1960), Pinter has provided simple stories, where the sequence of events forces the characters to new knowledge and activity but, because of the nature of this medium, Pinter could keep each episode short and vary the location or point of view very rapidly and so escape from too close a confinement to external cause and effect. In *The Homecoming,* as the title suggests, a number of encounters and adjustments arise naturally from a basic story; but here Pinter has used the various places of entry on his stage-set—from the road, the kitchen, the bedrooms and from Lenny's room—and the ability of characters to come and go, singly and in pairs or groups, so that with only two black-outs and one Act-interval the assembled family are constantly realigned with freedom and energy.

More important than story-line, for Pinter, is scope and occasion for his characters to work through, and work out, the potentialities of their beings and relationships. In *A Slight Ache* (1959–61), Edward and Flora are, for most of the play, simply left alone with the silent matchseller and so initiate every move and each new variation that will lead to their eventual separation and differing enslavements. In *Landscape* and *Silence* (1969), each character speaks his mind freely—as freely as his past, present and future seem to permit—without interruption and without sustained desire for communication. There is no event on stage, no entry or exit, except three small moves in the latter play, each ineffectual in that the positions at the end are identical to those at the beginning. Here, Pinter has found a way of making his characters speak or move only when their inner natures prompt them. His characters now seem to have free scope to express and, thereby, resolve or expend their personal and individual energies.

Clearly the shape of Pinter's plays depends above all on the potential of their characters, and on the dramatist's determination to show *them* determining a new relationship or new knowledge according to their own dynamism. This is how he talks of his task:

> I started off with this picture of the two people and let them carry on from there.[5]

> I like a feeling of order in what I write. . . . I have a pretty good idea of the course of events and I know the whereabouts it must stop, but I very rarely know how it is going to stop. All the preconceived notions I have are invariably wrong, for they are remedied by the characters in the writing. . . . Characters always grow out of all proportion to your original conception of them, and if they don't the play is a bad one.[6]

[5]"Writing for Myself," op. cit., 1008, p. 173.
[6]"Harold Pinter Replies," *New Theatre Magazine*, Vol. II, no. 2 (1961), p. 10.

Such a sense of engagement with their "material" can be found in many recent painters, such as Jackson Pollock:

> When I am *in* my painting, I'm not aware of what I'm doing. It is only after a sort of "get acquainted" period that I see what I have been about. I have no fears about making changes, destroying the image, etc., because the painting has a life of its own. I try to let it come through. It is only when I lose contact with the painting that the result is a mess. Otherwise there is pure harmony, an easy give and take, and the painting comes out well.[7]

This kind of artistic engagement depends on careful handling of detail and continuous awareness of possibility and achievement. But all this would achieve nothing if the original image, the characters and the configuration, was not powerful. It must be capable of leading the artist on to master, with difficulty, some significant experience or response to experience.

For Pinter, the relationship between himself and his dramatic material seems direct:

> I am objective in my selection and arrangement, but, as far as I'm concerned, my characters and I inhabit the same world. The only difference between them and me is that they don't arrange and select. I do the donkey work. But they carry the can. I think we're all in the same boat.[8]

Although he imagines the plays in action before him as he writes, he does not seem to see specific individuals. Rarely do his stage directions (or dialogue) give details of personal appearance, in the way that Bernard Shaw, Osborne or Wesker customarily explain height, weight, colour of hair, or manner of speaking. If Pinter imagines such details, so that he could recognize one of his characters off-stage, he does not consider the likeness important enough to tell his audience. For him, the salient points are sex and age, and that's the only lead he gives the audience. The published list of characters for *The Birthday Party* runs as follows:

[7]"My Painting," *Possibilities*, Vol. I (1947), p. 79.
[8]"Harold Pinter Replies," op. cit., p. 9.

Petey, a man in his sixties.

Meg, a woman in her sixties.

Stanley, a man in his late thirties.

Lulu, a girl in her twenties.

Goldberg, a man in his fifties.

McCann, a man of thirty.

The list for *The Homecoming* is similar, not even the relationship of Max to his sons, or to his brother, being mentioned.

Of course, family relationships will become apparent soon enough and they are clearly important bases for the writing of the play. (A page from an early draft of *The Homecoming*, reproduced in *Paris Review*,[9] shows that Max figured at this stage simply as "F," for Father, and Lenny as "3," for Third Son.) But it is necessary for Pinter's dramatic strategy that these essentials become apparent only in and through performance. In the same way, clothes, height and other physical characteristics are mentioned in dialogue when this is necessary, but such descriptions are not always accurate or consistent and, in any case, reveal at least as much about the speakers as about the persons described.

Reading Pinter's plays is to enter a curiously faceless world; to see them acted in different productions is to meet a single world that changes in all but certain mysterious aspects, of which modes of awareness and an inherent tendency towards being known more fully seem to be dominant. The "characters" as Pinter has indicated them in dialogue and stage-directions require substantiation: the actors do their share of this, but characters do not become clear until the audience has also begun to create them for themselves, piecing together hints, details, strangely various moments in which they express the cause of why they were thus and not otherwise.

The settings of the plays vary from fashionable to impoverished, from fanciful to brutally bare. The manners and apparent interests of the characters, the stage-business, the

[9]*Paris Review*, 39 (1966), p. 12.

lighting and supposed "weather" change likewise, often within a single play. But none of these details seems to nail a character down to any precisely confined range of behaviour. Flora, in *A Slight Ache,* can be a retiring wife, a gracious lady, a mother, a child and a mistress. Davies of *The Caretaker* is a tramp, sometimes speaking cockney and sometimes, possibly, Welsh; but at the end, his speech is simple, supplicatory, all but anonymous in its run on a few words and in its hesitations. There is consistency of rhythm and vocabulary in individual parts, and sometimes the social background seems consistent and solidly imagined; but these are not overriding considerations in the creation of character and action. In *The Homecoming,* when Teddy leaves his wife Ruth, she turns from business-like talk about prostitution to call him by a name not used before, "Eddie," and then "Don't become a stranger"—a phrase which seems to express dependence or concern, holds the future open and suggests possibilities about the past and her mode of understanding that are unexpected and out of the "key" of her role as a whole. She is not to be defined wholly by her obvious talents and her sustained manner of half-mocking speech.

Pinter's characters "inhabit the same world" as himself so that their reality is imaginary. Their strength and conviction depend on Pinter's sensitivity to the forces moving within them and not on his observation of physical facts or social environment. At the end of the play they are "finished," except as they go on living in the minds of the writer, the actors and the audience. So they belong in the theatre only, in that exploratory world where they have their only substantial existence. One cannot imagine them in relation to other characters or in other settings; and they have no activity which is not precisely necessary to the drama. They seem confined, even though presented in so many varying combinations and in so many apparently conflicting guises. They never speak to the audience; they often make jokes, but the audience overhears these and is not invited to enjoy them with the comic performer. The characters are there for our inspection, but, while Pinter has ways of drawing our precise attention, this is never demanded overtly, nor is it necessary for the play in performance. We have the unusual impression that we can come and go; indeed that some withdrawal is almost expected of us, so wholly private is the interrelated life of the characters, their activities and consciousness. His plays show private worlds: self-contained, obscure, "rather sexual," instinctive, irrational, frivolous perhaps—yet moving all the time until they have worked themselves out, until the subterfuge is expended and the interplay settled.

On the one hand Pinter has not given us pictures of "real life" and on the other he has not drawn us into a theatrical fantasy by splendid performances, challenging arguments or unavoidable statements. Rather he displays the reality of stage characters who at first seem alive only to himself, and who therefore have all the bafflement and complexity of his own mind—and the energy of that mind, which reaches forward and seeks to be "true." At the end of a performance, there is, perhaps, a sense of let-down, or anti-climax; for all the audience is left with is a mode of perception and a recognition of forces within characters that are clearly special, insubstantial, almost general. The great achievement of these plays is when the audience transfers this mode of perception from theatre to life; to this transference both the finish of the plays and the nature of their characters invite, by their own obvious limitations.

In Pinter's view, fantasy is at least as powerful in human motivation as rational thought or objective reality. All the plays show events, behaviour or settings that are outside the experience of any actual world. At first this element was expressed blatantly in stage-action: in *The Room,* Rose suddenly goes blind; in *The Birthday Party,* there are nightmare interrogations and Stanley suffers a physical metamorphosis; in *The Dumb Waiter,* fantastic orders are delivered and a cistern flushes as if by magic. In some plays written for television or radio the setting is fantastic, as in the changing furnishings of *The Basement* or the abundant blooms and the path to the monastery of *A Slight Ache.* In the latter play the silent match-seller is a character with almost no plausibility in any "real" world.

Where setting and events are close to the actual world, fantasy is present in speech and behaviour. In *The Dwarfs,* Len's imaginary, watching and ever-active creatures whom he talks about are obviously a fantasy of his mind and so, sometimes, are his conceptions of his friends, Pete and Mark, of the nurses in the hospital, of objects seen and touched. Pinter has realized the imaginary horrors springing from Len's distrust of activities and speech, and so in this play setting and incident only seldom and slightly depart from ordinary reality. In *The Caretaker,* written just before this, each of the three characters reacts to almost credible events in ways that show the imaginary gloss or distortion with which they view them. But here actions and speech are less directly fantastic, and often sound factual when they are not. (The clearest example is Aston's long speech about his experience in a mental hospital at the end of Act Two.) In *The Lover,* husband and wife actually act out their fantasies of being mistress and lover, dressing up and obviously pretending until, at the end, at least the outward charade is stopped. In *The Collection,* by keeping silent about what actually happened in Leeds, the two people who must know all, and the two who cannot know, with something of the same energy, express their own fantasies of what did happen; and, by the way, they also express their fantasies about themselves and their opposites in the four-sided confrontations.

By 1965, when *The Homecoming* was ready for production, Pinter had written two television plays, *A Night Out* and *Night School,* in which the fantasy was wholly restricted to personal reactions to events, all of which could be taken for actual and real, and are presented as such without ambiguity. The same may be said of the full-length stage-play, but the basic reactions of the characters here have a wholesale quality, a thoroughness of rejection or acceptance, that outstrips ordinary behaviour and so takes the play into fantasy while retaining an apparently unconfusing surface of ordinariness.

In *Landscape* and *Silence,* all speech directly reflects the thoughts of the characters. Events, objects and statements take on size, colour or power according to conscious and subconscious reactions. What is expressed is the interplay of fact and fantasy, the content of daydreams and self-indulgent thought. In *Silence* the setting is almost non-physical, Pinter asking only for *"Three areas. A chair in each area."* This play concentrates with the least conceivable distraction on what three characters, after some contact, can, and must, make of what they have been given by time and each other. The characters are separate and yet linked by what is now outside their control, a sequence of quite credible events. They can talk with each other, and even ask simple questions: but these sound like old interchanges, and in the wider and more sustained speeches each character is alone. At length they must rest in silence, in their unuttered fantasy and memory.[10]

For Pinter, fantasy and reality are inevitably mixed; this is the nature of the conscious life that theatre can reflect. Even in the earliest plays his handling of seemingly realistic details serves this view of life. He selects, emphasizes and controls in order to disclose the forces that exist within his characters, regardless of chance or human contact. For all the minutely defined details of everyday life that the audience perceives as if they were moments of actual human intercourse, the plays express the largest and most general issues of personal existence: fear and hope; defence and aggression; dependence and dominance; trust and withdrawal; helplessness and confidence; the objective, limited facts of living and its subjective, limitless potentialities; the child and the man; the male and female; the family and others; the self in all its various manifestations and in its essential confinement, in its intentions, deceptions and actual achievements as seen by others and as realized, imperfectly, by itself in actual being and in strange and for ever fugitive consciousness.

In *A Slight Ache,* man and wife meet an unknown, human derelict with a tray of damp and useless matches, in the setting of a garden and house on a gloriously fine midsummer's day. Edward has travelled to tropical regions and has speculated "for years," in his thoughts and writings, on primitive cultures and on space and time. He wakes with a "slight ache" on this

[10]Shortly before writing *Silence* Pinter acted in a television production of Sartre's *Huis Clos*; it is possible to see *Silence* as his version of death, or of life without the definement and curtailment of shared bodily existence.

day and meets, or thinks he meets, in the person of the matchseller whom he has observed for some time, a resistance to all easy evasions and polite gestures. So his own mind leads him to hear mockery and challenge, and to think of his own youth and training, of moonlight and the sea. Finally, he makes a desperate effort to understand his encounter and himself in a whispered "Who are you?," an unavailing move towards knowledge of a human being. The play changes from ordinary daily realism to a struggle with overwhelming fantasies and fears. Flora, the wife, begins irritated but sedate; she is careful of her husband, their house and "the garden." But by the end of her encounter with the matchseller, she is happily careful for the unknown visitor, whom she decisively calls Barnabas. The garden flowers are now "my japonica, my convolvulus. . . ." The "whole house" is polished, and she and the visitor walk hand-in-hand to the garden, as if entering a rediscovered innocence. She gives her husband the tray of matches, with "Here is your tray"; and she assumes command. The play is about abundant nature, possession, loss, service; about what is normally a "slight ache" in the head, and about a human encounter in a sun-filled garden and a cluttered home.

The Birthday Party intermixes reality and fantasy more thoroughly. For its basic action in three Acts Pinter relies on three main activities: a visit, a party and a departure. Each is calculated to arouse basic reactions from the characters, especially when the events are presented in a purposefully confusing way so that they all question what is happening or conceal their distrust by fantastic evasions. The party is avoided, accepted or elaborated by each character in his own fashion, as if each had a *divertissement* to create in some corporate dance. It is stage-managed by Pinter carefully, and he introduces odd occurrences without apology. So Goldberg and McCann have a game with an electric torch, that involves turning out the lights and shining the torch in the face of the "birthday boy," Stanley. A game of blind-man's-buff is extemporized at Lulu's suggestion. By these devices, Pinter makes darkness a recurrent element in the party and varies its effects. The light outside the room, and shining in the window when the lights are turned off, is at first *"faint"* (ed. 1960, p. 57); then it becomes *"fainter"* (p. 59); but when Stanley is blindfolded, catches Meg and begins to strangle her, there is a sudden *"blackout"* (p. 66) and this time Pinter directs, *"There is now no light at all through the window. The stage is in darkness."* In this darkness the torch is found and then lost, and then found again. The party is at its end and Stanley is discovered "spread-eagled" over Lulu on the table. Goldberg and McCann converge on him with the torch and he flattens himself against the wall, giggling furiously, when the curtain falls. This is obvious dramatic artifice—although Pinter does provide an excuse in explaining later that the shilling-in-the-slot electric meter had turned off the light at the crucial point. The fading daylight is controlled to work exactly in time with this. Pinter wants the party to end in darkness and violence, in a kind of death for Stanley, a confrontation with his two visitors in a small circle of light. He has been progressively isolated; his glasses have been removed and then broken, and his intended victims have been released. His reactions start submissively—his only words are near the beginning, asking politely for his glasses—and then the inarticulate responses are progressively wild, dangerous, clumsy, childish and help-less. For Stanley, the Birthday Party is a blind, furtive, dangerous struggle; he is alone and desperate; his response instinctive and final. Pinter uses the dramatist's power to invoke coincidence, to arrange the setting and, as it were, to choose the weapons, so that the guest of honour is down and out, his defences removed and his resources exposed.

When, for his departure in Act Three, Stanley is led silently into the room by McCann, he is dressed as if for a funeral; he is made to sit on a chair and McCann pronounces him "A new man" (p. 86). As Goldberg and McCann promise to "save him" and offer him "proper care and treatment," a free pass, re-orientation, success and many other attentions, Stanley remains quite still. When he is asked for a reply, he lifts his head "very slowly," clenches and unclenches his eyes, trembles, and finally emits a strange breathing sound. Then

[*They watch him. He draws a long breath which shudders down his body. He concentrates . . .*]

[*They watch. He concentrates. His head lowers, his chin draws into his chest, he crouches.*]   (p. 89)

Stanley is now in the foetal position, as at birth, and his responses are noises: "Uh-gughh" and "Caaahhh." He is twice asked his "opinion of the prospect," but

[*Stanley's body shudders, relaxes, his head drops, he becomes still again, stooped.*]

A few moments later he has to be helped out of his chair and moved towards the door, almost like a corpse, and so taken to Goldberg's waiting black car.

In these ways, Pinter has chosen events for *The Birthday Party* which involve the characters in a watch and a death, as well as in a kind of birth and remembrance. The words spoken support the dramatic metaphor, the associative extension from particular, almost ordinary circumstances and behaviour to a universal and wide arena for human effort. The gestures and stage-business support the metaphor by expressing the characters' physical and instinctive involvement. The final curtain marks the action as complete when the party is over and when the "party" who has been worked upon is taken away to a new life or death. The characters make their own clearest individual statements as the basic action is finished.

The basic action of *The Homecoming*, as for earlier plays, is marked by the ambiguous title: Teddy comes back to home; and leaves for his other home; Ruth comes to a new home; Joey "comes" (in a sexual sense) for Ruth, in his own home; Sam seems, at the end, to come to his "last home." For all the characters truths come home, and in the last silent moments of the play, centred on Ruth, with Max, the father, on his knees before her, a new home-circle is established.

Reality and fantasy are combined in the stage-setting which is, on the one hand, "An old house in North London," but on the other, a spacious hall or throne room. Pinter effects this double setting by an unusual direction:

A large room, extending the width of the stage.
The back wall, which contained the door, has been removed.
A square arch shape remains. Beyond it, the hall.

It is hard to imagine this structural alteration being made in any large, and already draughty, old house in North London; but for the play's action the effect is important.

It provides an arch, within the procenium arch of the theatre, "square" and therefore more vertical in emphasis than the broad rectangular stage-picture. This arch gives room for group entries and emphasizes the isolation of a lone watcher. It accentuates the height of the room and reveals a staircase going up to the bedrooms and a door to the street, and so it realizes the nature of each entry and exit more precisely. Above all, it gives visual emphasis and depth to the centre of the stage. The last static gathering will be backed by this inner arch, as if it were seen in a frame, so that set and actors together provide a last sculptural statement of homecoming.

The furniture is carefully chosen to accentuate this throne-room aspect of the living and entering space. There are "odd tables, chairs" but also "two large armchairs." A large sofa is placed off-centre to the left-hand side and against the right wall is a large sideboard. The dialogue clearly marks one of the chairs as belonging to the father, Max; the other, presumably belonged to the dead mother, Jessie. At the end of the play Max is not in his chair, but Ruth sits in what the stage-directions now call "her chair" (ed. 1966, pp. 81 and 82); this may be Max's or Jessie's, or one of the "odd chairs," now given a new, central significance.

During the course of the action, events usual in any home are elaborated in a way to command watchful attention, and move from the confinement of reality to the freedom and release of fantasy. With a slow deliberation, Lenny's provision of a glass of water for Ruth, and then for himself, defines a crucial encounter. These actions are part of a whole series involving preparation and acceptance of food and drink. Lenny's first attempt to question his father, Max, is to ask about the dinner he has cooked, and this leads to general resentment: "Why don't you buy a dog? You're a dog cook.

Honest. You think you're cooking for a lot of dogs" (p. 11).
Later Sam helps himself to an apple from the sideboard, with
a brief excuse, "Getting a bit peckish" (p. 16), and Max makes
no comment and no effort to provide. Immediately after this,
Joey enters and takes his jacket off, and, before he has sat
down, proclaims "Feel a big hungry" (p. 17); Sam agrees, but
now Max responds:

> Who do you think I am, your mother? Eh? Honest. They walk in
> here every time of the day and night like bloody animals. Go and
> find yourself a mother.

The next provisions of food and drink are the glasses of water
and, at the end of the Act in an early-morning episode, the
clearing-up of breakfast off-stage by Sam who simply enters
"with a cloth" and so provokes Max's scorn:

> You resent making my breakfast, that's what it is, isn't it? That's
> why you bang round the kitchen like that . . .   (p. 39)

Sam tries to hand the cloth to Max, but at this point Teddy and
Ruth come down the stairs and into the room. By this series of
episodes concerned with food and drink, Pinter has drawn
attention in the first Act to basic home-making activities, de-
fining his characters and leading on to other domestic rituals.
No meal is consumed on stage, in the manner of realistic plays
of home life, but this allows a greater variety of handling and a
more constant concern with these matters. Notably each
episode leads to a questioning of family relationships: Max as
father and mother; Ruth as stranger or mistress; Sam as
brother.

Act Two begins with an after-lunch ritual:

> *Max, Teddy, Lenny and Sam are about the stage, lighting cigars.*
> *Joey comes in from U.L. with a coffee tray, followed by Ruth. He puts the*
> *tray down. Ruth hands coffee to all the men. She sits with her cup. Max*
> *smiles at her.*
> Ruth. That was very good lunch.
> Max. I'm glad you liked it. [*To the others.*] Did you hear that? [*To*
> *Ruth.*] Well, I put my heart and soul into it, I can tell you. [*He*
> *sips.*] And this is a lovely cup of coffee.
> Ruth. I'm glad.
> [*Pause.*]

The silent business with cigars and coffee cups takes little time to read and to comprehend, but in action on the stage it is an elaborate and strange piece of business. Joey is not the most usual attendant, nor cigars their usual pleasure. Each of the six cups of coffee has to be poured and handed, and must therefore occupy an appreciable amount of time, during which no word is spoken. This fantastic dumb-show of polite acceptance is followed by Max's smile, who shortly before the end of Act One had greeted Ruth as an intruding whore. Mutual congratulations follow and Max is soon expatiating on his pleasure in seeing "the whole family" together again and on Jessie's virtues and the way he had pampered her:

> I remember the boys came down, in their pyjamas, all their hair shining, their faces pink, it was before they started shaving, and they knelt down at our feet, Jessie's and mine. I tell you, it was like Christmas.
> [*Pause.*]   (p. 46)

The feast is thus linked with images of a holy family. It looks forward, too, to the end of the play when all the boys except one, and Max himself, gather around the feet of Ruth, the new centre of the family. She has Joey's head in her lap and strokes his head; but there is now no food or drink.

Two more food and drink episodes precede the last tableau. The first is on Ruth's curt, "I'd like something to eat. [*To Lenny.*] I'd like a drink. Did you get any drink?" (p. 60). Whisky is provided by Lenny under Ruth's criticism, while Joey professes himself incapable of cooking. As the others accept the drinks and Joey "*moves closer to Ruth,*" Ruth disturbs the usual patterns by not answering Joey and by walking "*round the room.*" She now seems intent on getting Teddy, her husband, to speak of his "critical works." As he does this, he shows that he despises his family and he silently accepts the drink. The second episode follows a blackout as Teddy sits "*in his coat*" ready to go (p. 62). Lenny looks for a cheese-roll he has made for himself; he suspects Sam of taking it but Teddy coolly acknowledges the theft, in words which echo the talk over Ruth's glass of water: "I took your cheese-roll, Lenny," and later, "But I took it deliberately, Lenny." This gives occasion for Lenny to attack his brother, verbally, with memories of the past, scorn for the United States where he and Ruth now live, and apprehension of his father's death. The climax is Lenny's claim that the family, as he lives with it, does "make up a unit" (p. 66).

The rest of the play is concerned with home-making in more general and more precise ways. Joey rejoins the family after two hours with Ruth in bed. Max asks where "the whore" is (p. 69) and then proposes that Ruth should stay with them so that there is "a woman in the house." Teddy leaves and Ruth stays encouraging the fantasy proposals of the others that she should be set up in luxury as a prostitute near Greek Street. As Teddy is saying that Ruth will "Keep everyone company," Sam comes forward and announces that "Mac-Gregor had Jessie in the back of my cab as I drove them along." Having said this, he collapses (p. 79) and is left on the floor, not directly contradicted but condemned by Max for a "diseased imagination." The "home" seems to be breaking up and Teddy stands to go; with cheerful concern for the journey, brief farewells and Max's donation of a photograph of himself for Ted's boys, he has soon left. Ruth calls him back for a last word and then in silence, like the silence at the beginning of the Act, the characters realign themselves for the last family group around Ruth. She is the new provider who does not move to cook or bother to respond with words or anything else, other than a mechanical gesture:

> [*Teddy goes to the front door.*]
> *Ruth.* Eddie.
> [*Teddy turns.*]
> [*Pause.*]
> Don't become a stranger.
> [*Teddy goes, shuts the front door.*
> *Silence.*
> *The three men stand.*
> *Ruth sits relaxed in her chair.*
> *Sam lies still.*
> *Joey walks slowly across the room.*
> *He kneels at her chair.*
> *She touches his head, lightly.*
> *He puts his head in her lap.*

Max begins to move about them, backwards and forwards.
Max turns to Lenny.]

Max is the only one to speak now, and he soon falls to his knees and sobs like a child. Crawling past Sam's body, he looks up at Ruth:

[*He raises his face to her.*]
Kiss me.
[*She continues to touch Joey's head, lightly.*
Lenny stands, watching.]

CURTAIN

These are family gestures that complete the play, that show appetite and dependence: contact, withdrawal and submission in power or weakness.

Pinter has elaborated and controlled a sequence of normal-seeming events that carry a comparatively simple family story, but at the same time they are used to accentuate basic appetites, provisions and refusals. He starts with jocularity, petty quarrels and easy submissions, but moves towards cold confrontations and at last concludes with mutually sustained silence. The centre of the family in Max and the absent mother, Jessie, is continually marked by words; and, by showing the men providing food and drink for themselves, gestures and stage-business mark the changing positions and roles of provider and dependant. The stage-design and furniture accentuate the central sitting position, and the route of escape to bedroom or street; together they help to mark what is constant and what changing in the picture of Homecoming. The play stands or falls not by a plot or statement, but by the coherence of the episodes and the revelation of how, in events and behaviour, very like those ordinarily experienced by the audience, strong and repetitive forces work among male and female, within individuals and within a family.

This is the main progress of the play, but with it subsidiary explorations of character and relationships are made. There are self-concerned actions like Lenny's correction of his tie in front of a mirror or Joey's shadow-boxing. Some actions are obviously and blatantly meaningful, such as Lenny and

Ruth dancing slowly together, or Joey and Ruth rolling *"off the sofa on to the floor,"* as Max explains that he is talking about "a woman of feeling" (p. 60). But quite as much is expressed by a series of smaller, almost unremarkable activities: various kisses, handshakes, touches; putting on and off of clothes, entrances and exits, movements of sitting and standing, quiet responses of smiling or chuckling.

After watching the play, the audience's attention is attuned. Pinter has said nothing that is explicit and unambiguous about the basis of family life, of a mother's role, a brother's, a wife's, a child's, or about life outside the home affecting the home, but the audience has noticed how these elements of life operate within usual encounters and habits, and betray themselves to our understandings. He has also shown the characters all moving, with final ruthlessness and lack of self-regard, towards greater clarity and a finality of expression. This is, perhaps, the largest difference between the play and daily life; it is also the source of dramatic excitement, as Pinter slowly and stealthily reveals the interplay of his characters, and as he shares his own exploration. While the dramatic events are not progressively exciting, or optimistic, enjoyable, or pitiable, the dramatist's pursuit of an ending that has particular and corporate "truth" to all his invention does possess all these theatrical qualities, and his play, by the energy, danger and acuteness of its theatrical language, is able to transmit these to his audience.

The characters chosen by Pinter for each play are few in number and from a limited social range. They live in the present time only, without direct enactment of more than could be effected in an hour or two of real time. But if his dramatic material is thus limited, he presents it with compensating intensity. Everything is kept to a sharp minimum; in revision of his texts the main change is elimination, and in criticizing his early works he speaks of glibness or too many words.[11] His writing has an astringent athleticism that gives

[11]See revisions of *The Dwarfs* (1966 and 1968) and of *The Caretaker* (1962); his self-criticism is in *Paris Review*, Vol. 39 (1966), p. 26 and *Listener*, 6 November 1969.

his plays what is, perhaps, their rarest quality, a density and weight achieved without mass effects and without loss of excitement. Pinter's art is explorative and yet intense, restless and yet deliberate, related to ordinary talk and behaviour and yet releasing in powerful form the inner drives of his characters in final exposures that seem timeless and of general relevance.

The end of *The Homecoming* is like a group of statuary that the audience can encounter as it wishes. It is as massive, compulsive and generally eloquent as a silent *coup de théâtre* of Aeschylus, like Clytemnestra standing over the bodies of Agamemnon and Cassandra. The monumentality is achieved without a chorus; that perhaps is the role of the audience, for which Pinter has written no words. It is also found in characters who occupy the same time as the author and his audience, and not in figures from a mythical past.

This achievement seems to have come unsought. Pinter has followed his own sense of involvement in what immediately confronted him in his life and mind. He did not presume to create large figures of timeless relevance; rather his sense of "truth" in theatrical exploration of immediate experience has led him towards these mammoth and eloquent conclusions. Considering the effect his plays have in performance, I do not know whether to wonder more at Pinter's individual sensitivity and dedication, or at his use of the theatre's power to transform and heighten. My second thought is to remember that his art is precarious, depending wholly on the active involvement of the audience's conscious and subconscious mind.

Anti-Clockwise:
Betrayal in Performance

by Benedict Nightingale

Seen superficially, which is precisely how most of its reviewers have seen it, Harold Pinter's *Betrayal* is a piece of
shameless backsliding, a craven retreat to a theatrical period
when your average dramatist was obsessed with adulterous
husbands, "other" women, and triangles which, if not exactly
eternal, were certainly interminable. I mean, look at the plot.
In 1968 Jerry, a literary agent, makes a pass at his best friend's
wife, Emma. They begin an affair, and actually rent a flat for
their afternoon assignations. In 1973 the publisher-husband,
Robert, finds out about their liaison, which nevertheless takes
another two years to burn out. In 1977 Emma, who has by now
taken a novelist as lover, discovers that Robert has been ca-
noodling with woman after woman for years; and their marriage comes to a not-unexpected end. Yawn, fidget, scratch,
shrug: isn't a more original story to be found most nights at
the local Odeon?

But wait a moment. Whether or not Pinter backslides, his
new play positively backsomersaults. At any rate, it starts with
its chronological ending and ends with the sexual serenading
of its start. To an unsympathetic critic, this is at worst a cheesy
gimmick, at best an error which must drain the proceedings of
any tension the oaf Pinter might otherwise injected into them.
There is, however, a less damning way of interpreting his
preference for the anti-clockwise. It substitutes the question
"how?" for the cruder "what next?" in the minds of the audi-

ence. And in my view it deepens and darkens our perception
of the play, infecting the most innocent encounters with irony,
dread and a sense of doom.

To say, or imply, that a subject should be rejected because
it was once hackneyed seems to be thoroughly defeatist.
Clichés surely need to be reclaimed for reality; and by that test
Pinter's play is scarcely contemptible. It is all there: the instinctive evasions, the slips hurriedly corrected, the hollow questions ("and how is Emma?") to which the answer is already well
known, the faked offhandedness, the suspicion and paranoia
that the habit of deception tends to provoke in the mind of the
deceiver, the surreptitious *billets-doux,* the fear, the panic. As
the title confirms, the subject is not mainly the sexual aspects
of adultery. It is rather the mechanics of cheating, the politics
of betrayal. And there is, of course, more to the play than that.

Its reviewers, not content with coming glass-eyed and
woolly-eared to the theatre, have managed to sound inconsis-
tent as well. To some, Pinter is naïvely obvious, and to others
needlessly obscure. The truth is perhaps a bit subtler. He has
charted the bald facts of the situation with more than his usual
clarity, and then he has gone on to invite those of us with a
talent for emotional map-reading to use our energies more
creatively: we're to inspect and analyse the lightly-traced con-
tours of his characters, and speculate about those motives,
attitudes and feelings his cartography has left vague. Now,
there are objections to this as a dramatic practice, a few of
which I myself have put in the past. To shift the metaphor,
Pinter has sometimes earned a reputation for profundity simply by taking us to the edge of the psychological well and
pointing out its depth. He has allowed us to hear the echoes
rumbling up from inside, and even smell the rising stench, but
he has not often given us a direct, detailed look at the frogs,
tin-cans, used contraceptives, water-beetles, and all the rest of
the mess festering in the ooze at the bottom.

The general answer to this anxiety is, of course, that in
life, too, other people are commonly three-quarters hidden.
Most of us are doomed to spend our days in helpless emula-
tion of Pinter's audiences, delving for certainties that prove
elusive. The specific answer is that *Betrayal* does, in fact, offer

plenty of hints, glimpses, dabs of colour from which a profile can be built up, a state of consciousness inferred. Consider the case of Robert. Why, having been badly shaken by his accidental discovery of Emma's five-year-old affair, does he not stop it, and why doesn't he tell Jerry he has rumbled him? How can the two men soon afterwards lunch together in a restaurant, as they have done regularly for years, almost as if nothing has happened?

This particular scene, let me say, is classic Pinter, crammed with that tension the play has been accused of lacking. It has not, however, quite the anger and violence that is erupting just beneath the skin of both *The Collection* and *The Homecoming*. Partly, this is because these are sophisticated meritocrats, whose hostilities are obliquely expressed even by Pinter's standards of obliquity. Partly, Robert represses his outrage because, as an experienced if unadmitted adulterer himself, he has no moral standing in the case, probably could not survive close cross-examination, and is dubiously in love with Emma. But mainly, I think, he keeps mum because he genuinely cares for the nervous, fussy, hypochondriac chum who is betraying him. The most powerful relationship in the play is not between man and woman, but between man and man. It woul be glib to tack the word "homosexual" on to those loaded, pregnant exchanges from which, as it happens, the game of squash emerges as a recurrent metaphor for a special, rather sweaty intimacy. Better to talk of male bonding: a rapport demanding the attention of the zoologist as much as the psychologist. If the play is about disloyalty and deception, it is also about loyalty and friendship.

This contradiction makes the chronological close, which is actually scene two, particularly fascinating. Everybody, you recall, has been withholding vital information from everybody else. Jerry doesn't know that Robert knows, still less that Emma knows Robert knows; and when the truth hits him he is, as you would expect, seriously rattled at the thought of having been quietly tolerated by the best friend he spent seven years slyly wronging. In fact, he weeps. As he sees it, he's the victim of a "betrayal" at least as appalling as any he's committed. As Pinter sees it—well, Pinter being Pinter, he maintains his detachment, presents us with the evidence, and, here and elsewhere, leaves us to make what we may of it. What is surely indisputable, though, is that the dossier we end by taking to the jury-room is pretty elaborate, and remarkably suggestive about confused, shifting, silently screaming states of mind.

Peter Hall's production seems portentous at times, the result (perhaps) of excessive reverence for Pinter's celebrated pauses; but it still gets taut, watchful performances from Daniel Massey, Michael Gambon and Penelope Wilton, a trio who have had to put up with a maddening amount of critical sympathy, almost as if they were at a funeral. Let me insist, then, that this is not a sterile disaster. On the contrary, it is one of Pinter's more successful exercises in presenting the least and evoking the most. What looks flat commonly has fissures of feeling beneath it, and what sounds banal can be magnificently resonant. I don't think there's an idle word in the play. In fact, there's isn't a line that doesn't express desire, hurt, alarm, regret, rage or some concatenation of the impulses that are pounding about the slippery brainboxes of these artful dodgers. *Betrayal* is not a repository for mannered nothings; it is Pinter's *Golden Bowl,* a play of insight and assurance.

The Court and Its Favours:
The Careers of Christopher Hampton, David Storey, and John Arden

by Julian Hilton

I

From the beginning George Devine's policy was to make the Royal Court a writers' theatre: "Ours is not to be a producer's theatre or an actor's theatre; it is a writer's theatre." (*New Statesman,* 24 March, 1956) He wanted the Court to achieve two things for the writer: firstly that his play be put on under the best possible conditions, a chance usually denied the new writer at the start of his career, secondly to provide the writer with a workshop where he can test his ideas, even serve an apprenticeship, under skilled supervision. From 1956 to his death in 1966, Devine worked to discover and help new writers and he more than any other single figure in recent British theatre history has been responsible for a growing awareness of the need to repair relations between writers and theatres. But it is arguable just how far in practice such a policy can be realized. How many writers can a single theatre support to the required standard? How do you cope with the highly charged relationships between author, text, director and actors when several productions are in rehearsal simultaneously?

"The Court and Its Favours: The Careers of Christopher Hampton, David Storey, and John Arden." From Julian Hilton, "The Court and Its Favours," *Stratford-upon-Avon Studies, 19: Contemporary English Drama,* eds. Malcolm Bradbury and David Palmer [London: Edward Arnold (Publishers) Ltd., 1981], pp. 139–55. Copyright © 1981 Edward Arnold (Publishers) Ltd. Reprinted by permission of Edward Arnold (Publishers) Ltd. and Holmes & Meier Publishing Corp. (New York).

In this [essay] I shall be examining some of the work of John Arden, Christopher Hampton and David Storey. They form as diverse a group as one can imagine in modern British theatre yet have two things in common: they all started their careers as playwrights with the English Stage [Company] at the Court; and they are all concerned with the writer's place in society, a concern that perhaps stems in part from Devine's passionate commitment to the belief that a healthy state needs good theatres as much as good schools and hospitals.

II. *Christopher Hampton*

Like Devine himself, and indeed like Court directors Tony Richardson, William Gaskill and Lindsay Anderson, Christopher Hampton went to Oxford. After a most success-ful undergraduate career he began a happy relationship with the Court which culminated in his becoming its first official writer-in-residence. His duties were not new since they in-volved a large amount of script reading, which other writers like Arden had already done: but what was new was the official status, a measure of how far Devine's ideas had pene-trated Arts Council thinking on how subsidized theatre should function. Hampton's work shows many signs of his intellectual origins in its various ways of dealing with the problem of the relationship between artists and society. *When Did You Last See My Mother* (1966) has two school leavers waiting to go to Oxbridge; *The Philanthropist* (1970) presents the world to which they go; *Savages* (1973) contains a post-graduate student. In *Total Eclipse* (1969) the central figures are the artists Rimbaud and Verlaine; in *The Philanthropist* there is a playwright and a novelist. In *Savages,* West, the diplomat, is a poet and the whole Indian plot is conducted in a poetic mode. There is in both style and content a particular debt to the French dramatic tradition, which is perhaps not surprising in view of Hampton's modern language degree. This is clearest in his use of an epigraph from Molière's *Le Misanthrope* for *The Philanthropist,* whose tone and structure derive much from Molière.[1] But it is equally evident in his sense of drama as a medium of intellectual debate and exploration. Here the debt is both to modern writers like Sartre and the neoclassicism of Racine: Hampton draws from both an interest in purity of form and tightness of construction unusual in British drama. Most obviously this tightness expresses itself in his settings: these are nearly all interiors, some being literally small rooms, others small metaphorically.[2] Social and intellectual dominance is reflected in the physical domination of that space. Ian drives Jimmy from their shared flat; Philip is left alone in his university rooms; Verlaine lives in his wife's parents' house and is smothered by its middle-class values. The feelings of constriction and claustrophobia reach their most extreme form in the cell in which West is kept by his kidnapper Carlos, in which he is murdered and from which Carlos emerges only to be shot. There are never many people in these cells or boxes, and they seem to be trapped in them, like Philip, the philanthropist, himself. But although the box is constraining, an image perhaps of the cramped state of the Western mind, it also seems to stimulate art in a classic Freudian manner. Energy compressed and suppressed by the West releases itself either in art or violence or, often, both, as key scenes in all the plays show. Escape from the box appears to mean the end of one's career as a writer: Rimbaud "escapes" to the Middle East and runs guns (vicarious violence perhaps) but stops writing. All the plays show a tight, witty use of language and while there is little physical action there is much in the way of verbal battling to compensate.

When Did You Last See My Mother, staged while Hampton was still an undergraduate, and which, after two Sunday evening showings without decor, rapidly transferred to the West End, is a play founded on such confinements. In it two adolescents, Ian and Jimmy, share a claustrophobic London flat,

---

[1]Molière was in fact Hampton's special subject in his Oxford Finals. *Theatre Quarterly* Vol. III no. 12 (1973), p. 66.

[2]I am indebted to my colleague Tony Frost for this observation, as indeed for many ideas which have emerged in discussion with him of the authors I describe.

having previously shared a study at school. The action never leaves the room, and settles into a triangle of the two friends and Jimmy's mother, who sleeps with Ian as a substitute for her own son, whom she cannot reach. The tension clarifies the despair and contempt all three seem to feel, but the plot is schematic and psychologically unconvincing. But in any case Hampton is, however, not solely concerned with psychological naturalism, for the play also displays his preoccupation with theatre and theatricality, with fiction and fictionality. Ian, for example, tells in two forms a story about a lecture he has attended in Paris; the second account at the end of the play challenges the accuracy and truth of the first. The effect is theatrical and intellectual provocation, yet also an awkward but characteristic division in Hampton's attention, between naturalistic and fictionalist concerns. An apparently sincere emotional conflict is subverted by the new idea that one central character may be a pathological liar or an artist in manipulation; but we are then not sure how far to take our new awareness that truth in the play is in question.

The Philanthropist further develops this concern with challenging theatrical forms and conventions. If naturalistic plays like *Ivanov* gradually build up to suicide, Hampton here chooses to *begin* with one. But not before a remarkable use of anti-climax, another device Hampton had already displayed in his earlier play. The play starts with John, an undergraduate, in Philip's college room with his tutor, aptly named Don. John appears to break down, pulls out a revolver, puts it in his mouth, pulls the trigger, and nothing happens. It is an apparent joke; John is in fact reading the last scene of his play about which Don and Philip are unenthusiastic. However as a result of Philip's well-meant but clumsy and cutting comments, John repeats the scene and this time literally blows his brains out. Since the revolver is the same one it is not clear if the act is intentional or not, but either way the scene is a *tour de force* generating a whole series of "play-within-a-play" resonances. Like Ian's art-lecture story, a scene is presented, then represented with a different conclusion and the audience made to consider which of the layers of fiction, if any, is true. The parable is, however, taken a step further for at the very end of the play, when Philip has lost all his friends, he too takes out a revolver and puts it to his temple. As he pulls the trigger the gun becomes a cigarette lighter and the curtain falls (an anti-climax that surely cannot work off the page and must be seen).

Though most effective in performance, the intellectual problems this raises are similar to those in Ian's story. Does Philip lack the courage, or was his whole manner an act, an elaborate lie? Did he wish to "experience" suicide or was he playing with the audience? Hampton does, in other words, exploit the naturalistic convention of the removed fourth wall for all it is worth, and yet appears at the end to suggest that the whole exercise has been one in which the audience has been consciously manipulated by the actors. We are led by the action and the whole psychological motivation to believe Philip must kill himself, which he does not do. We are not told whether or not his decision to go on living is an acceptance of the constraints working on him and a vision of their necessity. The danger is that the short-term theatrical effectiveness of the anti-climax reduces the whole play in the long run to the one proposition that theatre is a lie.

That Hampton does not believe this is true is surely indicated by his next play, *Savages,* where the parable or poetic element takes up half the plot. West, a minor diplomat and minor poet, is kidnapped by Brazilian terrorists; this story is then interwoven with legends drawn and adapted from the various rituals of the "Quarup," an Indian festival of the dead that is linked closely with fertility rituals and seems to be offered as a model of a society where art, violence and sexuality are held in careful balance by ritual in a way now alien to Western man. It becomes evident that the savages are not the Indians but the speculators, the military governments, the well-meaning British and the urban terrorists. Both the kidnappers and the victim are trapped in their box and their only escape is death. Their constriction and oppression contrast strongly with the sunlight and space in which the Indians move, a concept hard to represent on stage, which is perhaps why, as Hampton indicates in his introduction, scenes were heavily cut for performance. The verse of the Indians is set off against the prose of the "Westerners" but while the idea of some lost capacity to harmonize the forces of life as an answer to European problems is seductive (and given literal representation in West's poems) it does not come across as effectively as it might in view of the very strongly naturalistic presentation of kidnap. West himself, and the West from which he comes, are in decline, boxed in and constricted. Even the constriction does not produce great art, though West does write in captivity and his death seems cruel if not particularly wasteful.

Once again Hampton cannot resist the ending that exposes all that we have seen as a lie. From the epigraph on, this time from Lévi-Strauss, and from his own passionate introduction about one of the great scandals of our time, we are invited to respond, both intellectually and emotionally, to the plight of the Indians, and quite rightly so. Then we learn at the end that more babies die in the slums of Brazil each year than all the Indians ever killed. Why, then, all the fuss about the Indians if their problems are relatively unimportant? And after all, according to Hampton, the Indians know better than the West how to live and die, and so should be better able to handle suffering than we.

Total Eclipse, Hampton's earlier and perhaps best play, deals with the relationship between two poets, Rimbaud and Verlaine, both of whom stopped writing; and does so in a way both satisfying as a character study and stimulating in the symbolic acts and gestures he uses to structure the work. The central themes are again art, violence and sexuality, and again all three are determined by constricting spaces: the elaborate French drawing room with its smotheringly bourgeois atmosphere, the seedy London lodging room, the Belgian prison; and the sequence is a neat downward progression. Violence is confined to a few moments but is the more powerful for being so: Verlaine punches his pregnant wife, and later shoots Rimbaud. Rimbaud responds in perhaps the most effective of all Hampton's uses of the dramatically repeated gesture. He comes into a cafe where Verlaine is drinking and cuts Verlaine's palms with a knife. At the very end he returns in a dream to Verlaine and, taking his hands, appears to be going to slash them again. Instead he kisses them with a delicacy that is both moving and brilliantly theatrical.

The key intellectual issue is why one writes and why one

stops writing. The answer for Verlaine seems relatively simple: he is brought up by the French middle class, made respectable, and given enough money for absinthe, so that he does not need to struggle and hence to write. His resistance to this smothering by comfort takes the form of odd violent outbursts, as we have seen, but it is also expressed in his initial invitation to the young Rimbaud, whom he had never met, to visit Paris. Rimbaud confronts him with the need to choose between sexual and financial ease and struggle, an opposition perhaps a little oversimplified but nevertheless crucial to the artist, perhaps even more so now in the days of pension funds and the welfare state. The more Verlaine drinks, the less he can write, but he needs to drink to quiet his conscience about not writing. Rimbaud's case is more complex, in that his art is more an act of exuberance, a channelling of his rich sexuality and violent temper into taut and intense form. He is not seduced by luxury, though he is perhaps unduly impressed for a while by Parisian bohemian life. But most obviously his life is a kind of art, of which writing is no more significant a part than making love or gun running. He stops because he no longer wants to write and it does not cause him the soul searching it causes Verlaine.

Rimbaud's returning to kiss Verlaine's palms is an unusually hopeful and conciliatory gesture for Hampton and is the one instance in his work where expectation is reversed without risking a violation of the coherence of form. It seems a pity there is not more of this hope in his other work—not hope for its own sake, but as a challenge to the mind apparently exhausted by the constrictions of its own limits; a mind so many of his central characters share.

III. *David Storey*

One of Devine's hopes was that writers whose social and educational background had not given them the entrée to the West End theatre world might be found and promoted by the Court. As it happens, Osborne, the first major Court discovery, was one such man, but there have been very few others.

David Storey, whose life on leaving school was split between professional rugby league and the Slade, was perhaps cast in this mould, but he, like many of the very early writers for the Court (e.g. Angus Wilson), came to it as an established novelist. More important, however, was the fact that it was Lindsay Anderson, who had been asked to direct the film of *This Sporting Life,* who brought Storey to the Court and subsequently directed most of his plays there. It is of course hard to assess the exact contribution made by a director in a long and fruitful working partnership like Storey's with Anderson, but the fact of the partnership (like Gaskill's with Bond or Hall's with Pinter) is vital both to an understanding of the workshop process in action at the Court and to an appreciation of Devine's philosophy of production as an ensemble activity, in which the writer was to be both a partner, and to some extent an amanuensis, to what is created in rehearsal.

It is perhaps too neat to see the rugby player and the artist at conflict in Storey, and that conflict expressing itself in writing: but Storey's interest in Nietzsche's early views, as expressed in *The Birth of Tragedy,* on tragic drama as the synthesis of Apollonian and Dionysian forces—forces of lyricism and linguistic creativity on the one hand against those of ecstatic movement on the other—does suggest that one of the keys to understanding his highly distinctive blend of the poetic and the naturalistic, and his concern for communal acts of a physical kind (team games or erecting tents), lies in the Nietzschean model. Nietzsche, unlike Freud, places the study of dreams in the Apollonian, conscious and rational part of the mind. The mind has the job of recovering and contemplating dream images which, if rightly interpreted, explain our actions and desires. Many of Storey's protagonists engage in this contemplative activity, though many do come increasingly to realize that in the process they have become alienated from society and from their families. Arnold Middleton, Steven, Reardon, Jack, Harry, Allott, all contemplate, but some have already gone mad in the process, and others are close to it. Against them are set those whose response is more physical and intuitive, father Shaw and his son Colin, the contractor Ewbank, and many of the team in *The Changing Room.* In all cases a study of behaviour is located within the Nietzschean, and ultimately Feuerbachian, vision of identity as being established through sexual, family and kinship ties, where the individual expresses himself in and through membership of, and loss of self in, a larger "communitas": indeed, he derives his nature from it.

There are in fact very few individuals in Storey's plays, but rather families or teams. The rooms in which they are shown are family spaces, like drawing-rooms, or shared spaces, like a changing-room, full of a continuous history of that group and its ancestors. Generations are frequently in conflict and the plays deal mostly with liminal moments in family evolution: marriages, anniversaries, home-comings after long absence and the upheavals associated with them. These respond well to simultaneous treatment on a naturalistic and a poetic level, and Storey's use of complex metaphors, like the erection and dismantling of a tent, do invite one to contemplation in the Apollonian manner. But the Dionysian side is equally important and indicates how difficult it is to recover Storey's meanings fully without seeing his plays staged. The contractor's gang, the rugby team, the life class and all the family gatherings bring relatively large numbers of actors onto the stage at once. As the characters they portray know each other well the dialogue between them is by no means confined to the verbal. Groups like rugby teams and working gangs develop, as a matter of course, close physical cooperation and their dialogue, like their threats, is as often physical as verbal. There is no way this sense of the simultaneity of words and actions and the complexity of meaning created in this way can be recovered from the page. This is perfectly consistent with the Nietzschean scheme: societal movement is Dionysian and must be witnessed and ideally participated in to be understood.

With the exception of *Arnold Middleton* (1967), we do not see the celebrations around which the early plays are set. Middleton is waiting for the return of his parents after ten years and throws a party, a "celebration," the day before their arrival. Their telegram to say they will not after all be coming triggers a breakdown in him. In *In Celebration* (1969) the

Shaws are celebrating their fortieth wedding anniversary and their three sons have returned home, curiously without their wives. The celebration is dinner at the top local hotel, but this occurs off stage. In *The Contractor* (1970) Ewbank's daughter is getting married, but we do not actually see the wedding or the reception that is held in the tent. In *The Changing Room* (1972) the main action of the play, the rugby game, goes on through-out, but is of course never seen. The result is that one is forced by Storey into considering why he so deliberately and often presents, as it were, the two outside panels of a triptych, but consciously removes the middle. The answer in part lies in the fact that he is shifting our attention from the "rites" and "celebrations" to the preparation for and the reactions to them, which in fact reveal more of the truth than the events themselves. But in part the structure derives from the logic of the Nietzschean model: the actual celebrations are Dionysian and therefore "abstract," like music, or beyond memory, like acts committed in drunken ecstasy. The artist knows these forces and is inspired by them, but does not, indeed cannot, describe them as they are an intrinsic part of life. His job is rather to recover images for contemplation from those areas of experience that operate on the conscious rather than un-conscious mind; that is, the "before" and "after" of familiar and societal ecstasies.

In this context the settings all have emblematic signifi-cance; the family sitting room becomes a sort of museum of family history, the store place of family wisdom. Articles in it, the typical knick-knacks, are all rich in association. A tent becomes, in its newness and size, both a huge extension of the white bridal gown and an image of "communitas," a womb, even, that bears a newly formed family. The intense scrutiny of family objects and the endless retelling of family history that always characterizes such events is also not that far re-moved from the process of investigation of the model in *Life Class*—and, as its title suggests, in that play Storey makes explicit the implication in his other works that everyone is an artist to the extent that he creates his own identity through contemplation of his past, at vital moments reassessing and even reshaping it. It is, however, a frequently violent process.

Middleton breaks down, as do, however briefly, most of the
Shaw family. Violence is never far from the surface in *The
Contractor,* though it is always controlled, for Storey makes it
clear from his comments on *In Celebration* that he does not see
any particular need to show violence as it is always present:

> In a way the explosion has already taken place, off or outside or
> away, and this is really the aftermath of battle. If you compare
> it with Ibsen in terms of approaching emotional realities, Ibsen
> is writing about what happened before the explosion: the
> bomb is festering away inside, and it does go off. *In Celebration*
> is after the bomb has shown what it can do. (*Drama,* Spring
> 1971)

Storey's own choice of violent images suggests a turbulent
mind, as does his use of the rather strange character Reardon
in *In Celebration,* whose apocalyptic visions of a whole world
burning seem oddly incompatible with the tense but far from
cataclysmic Shaw family row. Despite the upheavals and visions there are no deaths, few serious fights and the plays end
tranquilly if somewhat depressed or dazed in mood. In other
words, the Nietzschean logic, and indeed Storey's own description of the violence of the human condition, is not carried
through to its necessarily destructive conclusion. For Storey,
compromise and resignation are always possible, and when
Allott, the artist of *Life Class,* is confronted with the notion that
art may be destructive he appears with his ironizing "they tell
me," to retreat from the consequences: "Violation, they tell
me, is a prerequisite of art . . . disruption of prevailing values
. . . reintegration in another form entirely." (p. 89) The "other
form" is perhaps here the novel, Storey's other strength; but
in none of his plays does he go through with the complete
restructuring of experience and personality that his Nietzschean view of art suggests. Instead he closes the play with a
question about the role of the artist not through Allott's
mouth but through that of his pupil Saunders: "Perhaps there
isn't a role left for the artist . . . perhaps in an egalitarian
society—so-called—an artist is a liability . . . after all he's an
individual: he tells you by his gifts alone that all people can't be
equal. . . ." (London: Cape, ed., 1975, pp. 48–9). The artist
emerges then from this "life-class" as an Ubermensch, a

superior being by virtue of his art—a view that clearly conflicts with Storey's concern for social class, which is for him one of the chief causes of alienation in society. In *In Celebration,* for example, one of the chief tensions between the parents is that the mother is from the middle class and the father is a working-class miner. The family, therefore, is divided and uncertain about which class it belongs to. Ewbank, the contractor, is rich and an employer, but still working class; while his daughter, who is marrying a doctor, and his university educated son are clearly middle class in their attitudes. In *The Changing Room,* there is a less obvious class pattern, but a very clear metaphor of the alienation between labour and capital: the owner of the team has never watched a game in his life, yet exercises close control over his men. In its most extreme form the alienation of labour is expressed in the character Harry, whose whole life is the changing room but who has never in his life seen a game, the fruits of his labour. But in *Life Class* Storey himself is brought up against the central dilemma of the egalitarian socialist artist. The artist's talents are not ones in which all can share; they are not widely accessible even with the best educational opportunities.

In *Home,* the Storey–Anderson partnership perhaps reached its peak, for with Ralph Richardson and John Gielgud taking the lead roles the work had the optimum performance conditions Devine would have wished for it. Set in a mental hospital, where problems of class and socialist realism are less obviously important than in studies of coal miners, it achieves, especially in the superb first act, a remarkable blend of wit, Beckett-like lapidary dialogue and pathos:

Jack. Nice to see the sun again.
Harry. Very.
Jack. Been laid up for a few days.
Harry. Oh dear.
Jack. Chill. In bed.
Harry. Oh dear. Still . . . appreciate the comforts.
Jack. What? . . . You're right. Still . . . Nice to be out.
Harry. 'Tis.   (London: Cape ed., 1970, p. 10)

For a long time it is not clear that the play is set in an asylum, and it perhaps loses when the setting is made explicit. But, here, as indeed everywhere in Storey's plays, the central problem is one of communication, parents with children, bosses with men, teachers with pupils and, as here, people with themselves. Crises are provoked by broken communications consequent on the lack of a common language through which to talk and release aggression. This is why each man must in some degree be an artist, and above all one in language, for it is through language we define ourselves and what we see and experience about us. Nowhere is the failure of communication put more clearly than in an exchange from *Home,* structured like a typical two-man comic routine joke and yet as sharply ironic as anything in Storey's dialogue:

> *Kathleen.* I don't know what you're saying half the time. You
> realize that.
> *Harry.* Communication is a difficult factor.
> *Kathleen.* Say that again.   (p. 56)

Kathleen's reply is beautifully poised between her own inability to listen ("Say that again") and what could be an abbreviated form of affirmation ("You can say that again"). In its ambiguity and its sharpness the exchange reflects a delicacy in much of Storey's work that his comments about bombs and violence would seem to belie.

IV. *John Arden*

The range of John Arden's writing over twenty-five years is remarkable. He has written for major professional companies and the most inexperienced of amateurs, for the stage, television and radio; his style can be fiercely polemical and politically engaged, but also quiet and reflective, charged with metaphysical conceits; and he has explored a wide spectrum of staging techniques. His achievement is not, however, simply one of range, for in all his work there is that essential quality of critical self-appraisal that has kept his writing consistently fertile and challenging. In concluding his 1968 description of Arden's plays, Ronald Hayman lamented the fact that Arden had not by then found a company with which to work regularly, something he felt would not only have greatly enriched our national theatre but also been of benefit to Arden himself. Certainly when one considers the development of playwrights like Shakespeare, Molière and Brecht, this regular association with a single company seems of great benefit. Yet at the same time it may be that one source of Arden's inventiveness lies in the fact that, through his long-standing conflict with the theatre establishment, he has had to improvise and has never been able to rely on efficient professional staging to cover any deficiencies in his conceptions.

Strictly speaking, perhaps only three plays properly belong to a study of Court writing: *The Waters of Babylon* (1957), *Live Like Pigs* (1958) and *Sergeant Musgrave's Dance* (1959): A fourth, *The Happy Haven* (1960), first produced at Bristol University during a writing fellowship there, came to the Court; and *The Workhouse Donkey* (1963), which started off as a Court commission but was actually first seen at Chichester, may be counted a possible fifth. But while Arden's physical association with the Court ended in 1960, he—perhaps more than any other of Devine's initial circle of writers—has remained true to Devine's idea of the theatre as a workshop. In the Court plays one can see how Arden lays out the ground for his subsequent work, for certain early preoccupations have remained at the forefront of his mind. Yet then, as since, the main purpose of his plays has been to ask questions, not to answer them, and where answers have been offered for the most part they are tentative and formulated as yet further questions. This does not mean, however, that Arden is stuck in an intellectual treadmill, for one of the most exciting aspects of his *Non-Stop Connolly Show* (1975)—a cycle of six plays about the Irish labour leader Jim Connolly—is the way Arden's conviction that one of the fundamental "answers" lies in the dialectical nature of history, moving towards the inevitable triumph of the oppressed over the oppressor, informs the whole cycle with immense energy:

> We were the first to feel their loaded gun
> That would prevent us doing it any more—
> Or so they hope. We were the first. We shall not be the last.
> This was not history. It has not passed.
>   (London: Pluto Press ed., 1977-78, No.6, p. 106)

These words, which close the work, indicate the most important single theme in Arden's writing—the pursuit of what Ernst Bloch characterizes as *das Prinzip Hoffnung,* the principle of hope and optimism. This is not the glib socialist realist aesthetic that demands bright enthusiastic heroes of the revolution, free from doubts and thoughts of material prosperity, but a hard-won formulation of a moral, political and intellectual strategy of hope. Where Arden differs from the logic of Bloch's thought is that while Bloch's utopias must be presented in "concrete" and naturalistic shape, Arden's are accessible more through metaphor and implication.

Arden's background and education are in many respects a mixture of Hampton's and Storey's: born in Barnsley in 1930, he has in several of his plays drawn on his knowledge of life in the northeast. The sorts of community and politics he encountered there form the core of his long internal debate on the function of such closed societies and the role of artist and thinker within them. Equally important, however, was his university experience as a student of architecture, an art form which one might characterize as the art of applied ideas. Arden also sees applied ideas as the chief purpose of theatre, an aim he shares with Brecht: "We would emphasize finally that the play will work only if the actors are more concerned with undertaking the political arguments and implications of the story than with 'creating character' in the normal theatrical sense." This sort of statement, in fact part of the introduction to the *Non-Stop Connolly Show,* might well be taken as a general comment on how to approach Arden's work. Equally important, however, is his commitment to the business of writing itself, and this he owes to some extent to Devine. It was Devine who "rescued" him from a career as an architect and had faith enough in his work to allow it to lose large sums of money. It was his "writer's pass," Devine's system of allowing his writers access to the theatre at all times, that Arden counted his first great present in life:

> The other was a job reading manuscripts at a flat rate of a bob a script. I was accordingly able to leave the architect's office I was working in and spending all my time in or around a theatre.

The point is that the theatre had come out and asked me in. I don't suppose I would have ever really got going as a proper playwright if this had not happened.[3]

Not only therefore was the invitation to the Court of great significance to him, but the close and regular contact with it developed him as a writer. Arden is often concerned with reflective men, whose thoughts, however inarticulate, lead them to some sort of action. Arden's suspicion of intellectuals persists to this day, so it is important to see that thought is not necessarily for him the clear and logical activity required of the trained mind. Rather, men like Musgrave work, sometimes grope, through a mixture of images and intuitions towards some truth which, when they face it, they may baulk or not even recognize. The intellectuals, like Blomax in *The Workhouse Donkey*, David Lindsay in *Armstrong's Last Goodnight* (1964), and the poet himself in *The Bagman* (1971), all in some way discover the inadequacies of thought as compared with action, and the men of action like Musgrave, Butterfield, and King John, are portrayed as much more likeable and sincere if misguided or deluded men. The common pursuit of all these character studies is, however, towards a man who is both intellectually committed and capable of translating thought into action, and these virtues are united in Jim Connolly, who, like Lenin, could not only write a socialist paper but also fight for the cause. Connolly in fact loses his life for it, but in a way that gives Arden grounds for optimism.

Just how hard-won the optimism was is shown by the prevailing sense of disappointment in opportunities lost that all four Court plays have in common. Each one contains a number of figures who seem at first to be successful or wise or who have a message that is irresistible, but each one ends with the social, psychological or intellectual failure of their hopes and the sense that a vision of a better world embedded in the plays, is for the time being lost. Even in *Connolly* in fact the vision is apparently lost, but what is gained is the hope that the

[3]Quoted in Irving Wardle, *The Theatres of George Devine* (London: Cape, 1978), p. 199.

struggle is worthwhile. In *The Waters of Babylon*, the central
figure, Krank, is a rapacious landlord, exploiter of his friends
and veteran of a concentration camp extermination squad. As
his German name suggests, his devious mind is sick, but not in
a way that enables one to dismiss him as mad: rather his
cynicism confronts us with a question. Throughout the play
he has promised to reveal who he is, like the villain of some
melodrama; but in the end he does not:

> So many thousands of people
> In so large a cold field.
> How did they get into it?
> And what did they expect to find?
> (Harmondsworth: Penguin ed., 1964, pp. 96–7)

The cold field, with its suggestions of concentration camps, its
echoes of the storm scenes in *Lear* and feeling that it represents the total world, is a typically complex image: and the
closing question, echoing Christ talking to the disciples of
John the Baptist, then turns attention from the "many
thousands" back to the individual, who must, like John the
Baptist, ultimately make up his own mind as to what he believes. The agony and loneliness of having to make a decision
can only be borne if balanced by the overriding principle that
allows one to hope one is acting for the best.

  Live Like Pigs is similarly rich in complex images, the most
important of which are generated by the setting, the rooms of
a council house, and not the spoken text. The Sawneys are a
problem family, moved into a well cared-for council estate in
an attempt, through improving their living conditions, to
make them conform socially. The experiment is a disaster,
and they finally flee the house before the enraged neighbours
set fire to it, hoping to burn them all. (The play has assumed
an oddly prophetic note as three children were recently
burned to death on a council estate for similar reasons.) But
while it has a naturalistic aspect, dealing with the difficulties of
such social engineering, its metaphors yield other kinds of
meaning, ones located in particular rooms of the house,
which, rather like Storey's rooms, assume emblematic force.
The living room is the social space, the place of meeting and

conflict; the bedroom represents sexuality, feverishness and death. The stairs are not only the link between these experiences but also a place where the Sawneys drink. The bathroom, with its image of flowing water, represents both plenty and a profusion which becomes so rich as to overwhelm and drown this menace. The Sailor feels and articulates this menace as the neighbours close in at the end:

> You don't know this bastardy-like folk like I do. I've lived longer girl so listen. Aye, Aye, they live inside their hutches their houses and all. And they don't fight strong. But when they're out and calling you out, they don't run home soon, neither. They're in their crowd and they'll swarm you and drown.
>
> (Harmondsworth: Penguin ed., 1964, p. 175)

Here again the meanings are complex and even contradictory. The British middle classes, or the respectable working class, will, if provoked long enough, rouse themselves to fight and engulf their enemies. But in the tone there is both admiration for the spirit that defeated Hitler as well as dismay at the rejection of the Sawneys.

By far the best known play of this group is *Sergeant Musgrave's Dance,* produced in 1959. Like much of Arden's work, however, it appears to contain within it two contradictory styles and points of view. On the one hand, there is the real possibility that Musgrave's plan to hold a town to ransom with a new and dangerous weapon will work, will in fact spark off some sort of revolution among the disaffected colliers of the town. After all, it is no more absurd a prospect than a group of Bolsheviks declaring themselves to be the new rulers of Russia in October 1917 with little more support than Musgrave had to muster. On the other hand, Musgrave's failure to capitalize on the situation he creates seems both to confirm the elderly Marx's pessimism about the time-scale for the coming revolution, and also to demonstrate how thought—in this case Musgrave's sudden awareness of the ambiguity of violence— prevents action. In one sense this is a reflection of Arden's desire to be intellectually fair, to show both sides of the case: in another, it is simply being honest to history. Here he is most obviously at odds with socialist realist aesthetics, which would

demand some sort of triumphant vision of success from Musgrave rather than the bewildered steps towards the gallows
which close the play. But he also refuses to simplify issues in a
way demanded by socialist realism: when at the end of the play
Musgrave is hesitating, it is not because his anger evaporates
or his vision of the evils of imperialist capitalism in any way
diminishes but because he cannot be sure that those people he
has lined up in front of his gun are guilty of creating such a
system. Are they not also innocents, like Billy Hicks whose
skeleton he has displayed above the market place? This is just
the difficulty Marx had to face, for it is the fact that in a
revolution it is invariably the oppressed who suffer most,
which places severe moral constraints on any would-be revolutionary. The resolution of the play's opposed views lies in a
strong implicit demand for pacific protest. Musgrave's gun,
pointed, as it is, not just at the on-stage audience but at the
auditorium, must suggest immense destructive potential,
even nuclear threat. What holds Musgrave's hand at the end is
a vision that, once started, violence would destroy the whole
race, a perception that the glorious societal recruiting dance
of the middle of the play is only the first movement in a dance
that ends in death. This is, then, a weakness in Nietzsche's
idealized vision of the Dionysian ecstasy-destroying self, that it
has, built within it, loss of control, surrender of moral values,
of the sort that overtook fascist Europe in the 1930s and led to
the Second World War.

Early critical incomprehension of *Musgrave* stemmed
largely, however, from its mixture of styles—seen as a fault in
the first two plays as well. What appears to be a naturalistic
work about soldiers and colliers is also a poetic dance of death,
and a series of political statements about imperialism. All
these themes have their commensurate linguistic registers—
plain north-country dialect for the colliers contemplating
strike action, Musgrave's rich imagery and Sparky's haunting
songs—but none of these on its own seems to offer a complete
picture. Arden's answer, of course, was that he was not attempting any unity, that the whole point of his experiment lay
in the diversity of theme and language and the tensions that
engendered, and for this very reason he achieves the Brecht-

ian ideal of getting his audiences to think about his ideas rather than about his characters.

Though *Musgrave* was actually the last wholly Court piece, his next major work, *The Workhouse Donkey,* started off as a Court commission. The idea was

> for the audience to come and go throughout the performance, assisted perhaps by a printed synopsis of the play from which they could deduce those scenes or episodes which would interest them particularly, and those they could afford to miss. A theatre presenting such an entertainment would, of course, need to offer rival attractions as well and would in fact take on some of the characteristics of a fairground or park.
>
> (London: Methuen, ed., 1964, Intro. p. 8)

The constraints of the Chichester festival stage and resources, the demands of the Lord Chamberlain and Arden's own problems made the final version, both as performed and published, remote from the original drafts, but it does point to the essential difficulty about Arden's work as published, that so much of its effect depends on the staging, the use of scenery, costume, props, of music and dance that the printed text can at best be only an indication of what the theatrical experience is like. In this he shows himself closest to one of the major influences on him, Ben Jonson, and in particular Jonson's *Bartholomew Fair.* One of the decisive experiences for Arden was, by his own account in *To Present the Pretence,* the 1950 Edinburgh festival production by George Devine of *Bartholomew Fair*: "the main impression I retain is of having actually *been at a fair* (rather than having seen a play about some fictional people at a fair). . . ."[4] The writer himself is a craftsman come to sell his wares like any other skilled artisan. The importance of this for an understanding of Arden's political attitude is that writing for the stage is seen as a pre-capitalist form of labour: the worker is not alienated from the product of his labour but remains in contact with it from conception to execution.

Set, like *Musgrave,* in the north, in a tight, "closed," community, *The Workhouse Donkey* describes the fall of ex-mayor

---

[4]*To Present the Pretence* (London: Methuen, 1977), p. 32.

Charlie Butterthwaite from "Napoleon" of the town to an outcast. The agent of the fall is the "intellectual" Colonel Feng, the new head of police whose uncompromisingly strict sense of public morality leads to his own fall as well, leaving the field clear for the capitalists to regain control of the town they had lost. In a sense, Butterthwaite is like Musgrave, and his grip on the local community an indication of where Musgrave might have reached had he been more decisive.

The scene which focuses the play's problems comes when Butterthwaite, deeply in debt to his machiavellian adviser, Dr. Blomax, decides to steal the outstanding money from the council safe. In naturalistic terms this is not that plausible a move for an astute politician, though it does reveal Butterthwaite's arrogance reaching maniacal proportions; much more important is the information it offers about Arden's nature as a writer, one which is both Jonsonian and Swiftian. The artist's role is to be the conscience of society, a thorn in the flesh: he is both caustic and scurrilous; he may opt for simultaneous use of naturalistic and imagistic modes, a technique one finds in *Gulliver's Travels.* Indeed the image of the donkey itself has both these levels, as Butterthwaite's song makes clear:

> Oh what a shock, I nearly died,
> I saw my ears as small as these,
> Two feet, two hands, a pair of knees,
> My eyeballs jumped from side to side,
> I jumped right round. I bawled out loud,
> You lousy liars, I've found you out!
> I know now why you're fleeing . . .
> I am no donkey never was,
> I'm a naked human being.
>
> (London: Methuen, ed., 1964, p. 99)

Like Krank's closing questions, Butterthwaite's song is rich and resonant. The sudden shock of recognition is structurally presented like a conceit, whose force, as Donne said, was left to the "shutting up." It is also a similar shock to the one Gulliver tries to ward off when he begins to sense that he too is a Yahoo, though Arden's optimism makes him see the recognition as a positive acceptance of being human in a way Gulliver always resists. But the resonances are also tragic, in the fulfilling sense of tragedy that Nietzsche identifies in Oedipus's question "who am I?" The point of the tragic experience is to make everyone ask who he is: but where Nietzsche's answer is aesthetic, "I am my art," Arden's is more political, "I'm a naked human being." All privilege and class advantage is, in other words, a fiction of the rich.

Arden's concern with the writer's role in society comes to a head in two works stemming from the late 1960s, *The Bagman,* his short and intensely personal radio play, and the huge cycle of three plays grouped under the heading, *The Island of the Mighty* (1974). The total failure of relations between Arden and the Royal Shakespeare Company over the latter led to Arden and Margaretta D'Arcy picketing the production as a result of what they saw as a recreation of the idea, by the director, in a spirit totally alien to their conception. The Ardens give their side of the story at some length in *To Present the Pretence* (1977) which, apart from anything else, shows just how important to Arden's sense of his work the precise details of staging are. But the whole episode marks what was perhaps the lowest point in his dealings with the "Establishment." The plays themselves explore, through the Arthurian legends in their early Celtic form, the relations between the artist and poet (like Merlin) and the state. Merlin is brilliant but dishonest, and his dishonesty leads him to disaster and madness. While one cannot read a precise psychogram from this, there is no doubt that Arden puts much of himself into Merlin, arguing with himself over whether the poet should have a place in society or be locked in a cave like Merlin; and, if he should have a place, whether it is right that he play conscience to the state. Much tauter, and more incisive, is his analogous analysis of the same issues in *The Bagman,* a first-person narrative poem where Arden has a brief experience of the sort of encounters Swift created for Gulliver.

Once again the mood is one of Oedipal questioning: who am I? If I am my art, what will people make of it?

> If on this soggy Thursday, I should fall down dead,
> What of my life and death would then be said?

"He covered sheets of paper with his babble,
He covered yards of stage-cloth with invented people,
He worked alone for years yet was not able
To chase a little rat from underneath the table."
              (Harmondsworth: Penguin ed., 1964, pp. 37–38)

Arden falls asleep and in a dream buys a mysterious bag from
an old crone. In the bag are figures who perform, without
prompting, exactly what their audiences wish to see. The
people want hints of revolution, but only hints: the nobility
want sex-shows, and new ones every night. This is of course a
well deserved attack on the staple diet of West End audiences,
but it also raises questions directed at himself. These come to a
head when he is kidnapped in the dream by terrorists. When
he opens the bag for the figures to perform they refuse,
knowing that:

Men of war do not require
To see themselves in a truthful mirror
All that they need to spur them to action
Is their own most bloody reflection
In the white eyeballs of their fire.   (p. 86)

The moral, therefore, for the writer is to *do* more, and yet also
to realize that writing is, if rightly approached, an act as well.
The writer is as able to fight for the cause as the man of action
because writing is action. Out of this realization grew the
Connolly cycle.

The première of the *Non-Stop Connolly Show* took place in
Dublin over Easter 1975, in celebration of the anniversary of
the 1916 rising. A further measure of the extent of the breach
between Arden and the "Establishment" was the fact that the
event passed almost unnoticed and the plays—despite being
perhaps the single most impressive achievement of the British
theatre in the 70s—are still unknown. There are six in all,
based around the life of Jim Connolly, his talents as thinker
and organizer of labour, his trip to America, his contacts with
international socialism and his martyr's death at the hands of
the British government. The style is a remarkable blend of
melodrama, living newspaper, political propaganda and
music hall, all bound up in an historical sweep of world-

historical proportions. Connolly himself may not be the Hegelian figure who moves history, but the issues which he symbolizes are. His adversary, the all-purpose pantomime villain, is the capitalist Grabitall, but the melodramatic shape he is given intensifies rather than diminishes his menace. The show is avowedly emblematic, requiring: "stylized, easily changed, strongly-defined costumes and possibly stock masks for recurrent social types."

The success of the work depends substantially on two factors, Connolly himself, and the staging. In Connolly, Arden for the first time chose a protagonist who was writer and thinker and a man of action, and also one whose conduct he could endorse: as such, he grew directly out of the conclusions Arden had drawn from *The Bagman,* a writer whose words were also deeds. Connolly also has the Bagman's power to look at himself with witty detachment; he returns home one day after selling newspapers in the cold and explains that to be an activist "you must wear woollen gloves upon each fist." (no. 2, p. 49) This double aspect to the joke reflects Arden's confidence in his hero: even the most fiery activist needs woollen gloves to keep warm, but also to soften the blow to their adversary. It is as if the violent solution that Musgrave contemplated is here finally rejected.

The staging has much in common with rapid cross-cutting techniques of film. Characters come and go quickly and are usually only figuratively represented. This places great demands on the actors, of course, not least on their stamina: but more importantly it captures the feeling of history being made. It suggests an uncanny feeling that fragmentation and myriad-mindedness offer a truer reflection of how the individual experiences history than any great holistic theory: and yet, through the vision of men like Connolly, the organizing principle can be glimpsed. Here perhaps is the role of the artist, and one that seems almost Aristotelian in concept: the artist can organize, recreate and represent history in a way that makes us realize that history is not safely located in the past. Because what Connolly was trying to do still has to be done, he is not past. The artist sees this truth and finds a way to present it. The key difference between Aristotle's and Arden's view of the artist lies, however, in their understanding of what type of experience he examines. Oedipus is a man on his own, and the questions he asks emphasize his individuality and particularity. True, he stands metaphorically for us all, but he is still an individual. Connolly, by contrast, is a product of a particular society, and what is shown is not his individual efforts but the society he is trying to reform. Where Aristotle sees poetry as embracing and containing history, Arden sees only the immediacy of history and its specificity. This is why it is "non-stop," a structural rejection of the Aristotelian principles of "beginning, middle and end" in favour of the continuing movement of history.

V

Even though early critics were puzzled by Arden, they recognized that whatever he did he took them along with him. This is still true, for Arden has the great writer's ability to demand of his reader or audience that he listen, even when his tale appears as erratic and bewildering as the Ancient Mariner's. Arden has not created a character more striking than Musgrave, but that is largely because Musgrave was the last *character* in a naturalistic sense that he tried to create—and even then character was only part of the purpose. But that is perhaps one major reason why Arden is still known essentially for one play. British audiences, with the same suspicion of "ideas" in art than enraged Mathew Arnold, resist what they feel may be the preacher in Arden. Storey and Hampton, by contrast, who do appear to create characters, have as a result fared rather better than Arden in terms of popular esteem, because for all their interest in stylistic experiments and in breaking naturalistic modes of writing still they use naturalism enough for audiences not to feel bewildered or insulted. Arden is not the first writer this century to write in exile, and exile does contribute some of the passion with which he writes. Yet it would be a great day for British theatre in the 1980s if another George Devine could be found to go out and ask Arden back into his theatre.

Form and Style
in the Plays of Joe Orton

by Katharine J. Worth

Victorian notes still sound quite strongly in the plays of
Joe Orton, the most accomplished and witty of present-day
practitioners in the genre. His tragic death when his powers
were just maturing was a great loss to the English theatre.
Partly it's his preoccupation with clergymen and policemen
that links him with his Victorian predecessors. These are both
types of more ancient lineage certainly, but a nineteenth century odour of sanctity does seem to hang about the clergymen.
One hears the echoes of fruity voices—Wilde's Canon Chasuble (My metaphor was drawn from bees), Pinero's sporting
Dean (What dreadful wave threatens to engulf the
Deanery?)—behind the bland tones of the maniac clergymen
in *Funeral Games*. There's a note of Lewis Carroll too:

> What shape is your hot water bottle?
> I haven't got one.
> Too proud. Mine takes the form of a cross. There's piety for you.

But the macabre vision of the hot water bottle cross pulls one
up short: this is certainly a new twist to the family likeness, an
unlooked for, formidable regrouping of the genes.

I suppose it is this power of his to shock and offend
susceptibilities that first comes to mind when Orton is named.
He goes in such a head-on way for taboos and sacred areas of
all kinds. One of Winston Churchill's missing parts turns up in

a cigar box (double take here, it *is* a cigar); psychiatrists compete madly to certify each other, clergymen murder their erring wives to demonstrate to their flock their soundness on the seventh commandment; a son takes over his mother's coffin to hide stolen goods in and ends up playing horrific funeral games with the corpse, spilling false eyes and teeth all over the stage. "Your sense of detachment is terrifying, lad," says the Inspector, "Most people would at least flinch upon seeing their mother's eyes and teeth handed around like nuts at Christmas." Orton's characters don't, but his audience presumably do: if they don't, the farce hasn't really served its purpose; the worst fears, the most nightmarish anxieties haven't been given the airing he offers. As in nightmares, ideas keep turning into their opposites on his stage. It's always the clergyman who is the lecherous killer, the policeman—who starts off seeming a solid Dr. Watson figure (You must have realized by now, sir, that I am not from the Water Board)— who turns out to be the most adept in corruption.

It's rather curious to find this dream subversiveness sometimes taken by critics firmly towards social commentary,[1] a spur to social conscience rather than as one might have thought, a diabolical sort of holiday from it. There are topical allusions in the plays, certainly, but they seem to function on the whole in a traditional way of farce as antidote; like Alice's little bottle marked "Drink me" they change the perspective alarmingly, might even turn out to be poison, but the final effect is wonderfully freeing. "Health is the primary duty of life," said Wilde's Lady Bracknell. Orton's farces seem to be playing that game, working out dark fantasies in extravagant cosmic terms that both express and exorcize them.

He is arrestingly original in his ability to push the dark elements so much to the fore without losing that sense of health. Some of the risks he takes do almost but not quite

[1]John Lahr, for instance draws some precise social morals, comparing Inspector Truscott with Spiro Agnew and Doctor Rance with the Nixon administration in his interesting article, "Artist of the Outrageous," reprinted from *Evergreen Review* as introduction to *What the Butler Saw* (New York 1969).

shatter the convention. In *Funeral Games*, for instance, there's a disturbing moment when Tessa, bound to a chair, is being threatened by the two mad clergymen and it seems that after all murder might be a real possibility just when we've got used to thinking of it as an abstract affair of macabre comic props like the hand chopped off at the wrist (it turns out not to be real) and bad taste jokes about dead bodies—"She's under a ton of smokeless. I got it at the reduced summer rate." And his handling of the comic nemesis is worrying, too. One thinks of Wilde's saying—"Life is so terribly deficient in form. The catastrophes happen in the wrong way and to the wrong people." Farce normally corrects that deficiency with a very strict nemesis. On Orton's stage, though, the most harmless characters tend to have the worst time sometimes right to the end. It's certainly disturbing when *Loot* ends with the corrupt policeman joining forces with the thieves (one of whom is supposedly a multiple murderer), while McLeavy who knows nothing whatever about what has been going on is dragged off shouting "I'm innocent! I'm innocent!" and the others look ahead to the "accidental" death in prison that will tie everything up for them.

It's a daring departure from the farcical norm to leave us suspended in the dream, on the other side of the looking glass: the effect is unsettling. But although the incidents aren't reassuring the tone and the gargantuan exaggerations are: Truscott saying carelessly "Oh, anything will do" when he's asked what he'll charge McLeavy with, Fay making everything cosy for Hal—"We'll bury your father with your mother. That will be nice for him, won't it?," and McLeavy himself, absurdly lamenting as he's led off, "Oh, what a terrible thing to happen to a man who's been kissed by the Pope."

Orton's skill in keeping his situations delicately balanced between real life and fantasy, daylight and dream can be seen developing steadily, it seems to me,[2] between his first play, *Entertaining Mr. Sloane* and the posthumous *What the Butler*

---

[2]For one of Orton's critics, J. R. Taylor, the reverse is true. He finds *Loot* less satisfactory than *Entertaining Mr. Sloane* "because the balance has shifted slightly in the direction of farce," *The Second Wave*, 1971, p. 131.

Saw. Entertaining Mr. Sloane is cast on more Pinteresque lines
than the later plays: its terms are too human, the mechanism is
too slow, to let us take the characters as figures of farce, and
yet the central events, the brutal mishandling of the old man
and the sexual blackmail that follows, are presented with a
kind of unyielding comic aplomb that undercuts human responses and raises worrying doubts about the playwright's
own sympathies. It's hard to avoid ordinary human uneasi-
ness about Mr. Sloane's attack on Kemp: there's too strong a
feeling of real pain and fear in it to allow the detachment
Orton seems to invite with his tough jokes and his cool handling of the manslaughter (as it proves to be).

In *Loot* the cool convention is much more firmly established. "It's a theme which less skillfully handled could've
given offence," Truscott says to Fay, complimenting her on
the direct, simple style of her murder confession. Style does
have this sort of vital function in the play, not to prevent
offence exactly, but to keep feeling in its place. There is still a
good deal of physical brutality: Truscott getting Hal on the
floor and kicking him isn't a pleasant sight. But it's kept at a
careful distance, partly by being taken so fast, partly by the
jauntiness of the dialogue at the receiving end of the violence.
Whereas old Kemp lets out realistic cries of pain and calls for
his son—"I want Ed"—Hal comes back with repartee:

> *Truscott.* Under any other political system I'd have you on the
> floor in tears.
> *Hal.* You've got me on the floor in tears.

So long as the victims can keep their end up with this sort
of stoical calm we can keep up our detachment too. It's rather
harder in a way where the corpse is concerned—no chance for
repartee there—but Orton finds other means; he stresses the
artificial elements—the glass eyes of the wrong colour, for
instance—until the corpse finally comes to seem very little
different from the dressmaker's dummy that is substituted for
it at one point in the frantic game of hunt the treasure it is
caught up in.

The technique is assured in *Loot* but there are rough notes
in the play that keep it more earthbound than Orton's last

full-length work, *What the Butler Saw*. Here his control of his anarchic material reaches its high point. There's a blend of steel and airiness about it that brings Wilde irresistibly to mind, remarkably really, considering how outrageously physical in vulgar picture postcard style Orton's farce is, how much closer in some ways to the Aldwych tradition or to French sex farce than to the ethereally refined version Wilde arrived at in *The Importance of Being Earnest*.

Trousers come off with grotesque regularity in *What the Butler Saw*: half the characters are half naked most of the time. The command, "Undress and lie on the couch" rings maniacally through the action; starting as a simple (if unorthodox) start of a seduction and ending as a hysterically funny and desperate expression of the total bafflement about sexual identity that finally enwraps the characters.

And yet despite the picture postcard grossness, a demure note is beautifully kept up:

> Two young people / One mad and one sexually insatiable / both naked, are roaming this house. At all costs we must prevent a collision.

The content belongs to Orton's world but the style wouldn't be out of place in Wilde's; it's rather how Canon Chasuble might put it, one feels, if he were to run out of metaphor.

There are other similarities with *The Importance of Being Earnest*: the plots are in fact strikingly close at crucial points.[3] Wilde's plot turns on the double identity of Jack and Algernon and the emergence of Jack's other self "Ernest" as the mythical being whom practically everyone in the play is pursuing or trying to be. Orton works out a vastly more complicated version of this identity theme in *What the Butler Saw*. We begin with a single self, a simple secretary, Geraldine Barclay, who sets things going when she applies for a post as secretary in Dr. Prentice's psychiatric clinic. Out of his abortive attempt to seduce her (which she never appears to understand) comes

---

[3] In an interview in *Transatlantic Review* 24, Orton spoke of his admiration for Wilde and his wish to write a play as good as *The Importance of Being Earnest*.

the struggle to hide her from his wife and the wild game of hide and seek in which Geraldine Barclay begins to break up into a number of different selves.

Geraldine palpitates nakedly on stage while Miss Barclay, the missing secretary, is hunted by the psychiatrist's wife, the rival psychiatrist and a policeman. Geraldine—frantically on the lookout for clothes to put on—takes shelter in the identity of Nick Beckett, the pageboy, and then under pressure of the chase creates an alter ego for him too, Gerald Barclay, his imaginary brother. So two mythical free floating beings take shape for the "real" characters to go in and out of. As Wilde's Algernon steals the identity of Ernest, so Nick and Geraldine steal each other's secondary identities. She vanishes into a shape with cropped hair and boy's clothes, he into a woman's dress, blonde wig and "low cultured voice" to match. Getting rid of the alter ego, as in Wilde's play, proves more difficult than creating it: an attempt to kill off the surplus personalities leads into monstrous new growths, till Dr. Prentice— desperately trying to get rid of women's shoes in flower vases and drugged bodies in the garden—comes to be seen as "a transvestite, fetishist bi-sexual murderer."

Again as in Wilde's play, the crowning joke comes at the end when the invented identities turn out to be after all, the true ones. There really are twin selves, a Geraldine and Gerald, who were conceived in the linen cupboard at the Station Hotel, that off stage dream area—equivalent to the handbag in *The Importance of Being Earnest*—associated with sexual orgies, illegitimacy, the pleasure principle unrestrained. Here Mrs. Prentice pursues Platonic dreams—"I went to the linen cupboard ... hoping to find a chambermaid"—and enjoys fantasies of being sexually assaulted, fantasies in which objects like handbags have a strangely prominent place—"When I repulsed him he attempted to rape me. I fought him off but not before he'd stolen my handbag and several articles of clothing."

The final recognition scene introduces new dark notes into these adventures. Mrs. Prentice's claim to have been assaulted by Nick and Dr. Prentice's attempt to seduce Geraldine become rather disturbing when Nick and Geraldine are revealed as their lost twin children, fruit of a "real" rape in the linen cupboard. Not that there's any danger of our seeing it in real life terms—who could take the linen cupboard seriously!—but the fantasies are peculiarly vivid: we do see Geraldine on the couch and throwing her clothes out from behind the curtain. In a way, the loathly Dr. Rance is proved right:

> If you are this child's father my book can be written in good faith—she *is* the victim of an incestuous assault!

Rance, however is the great warning against our taking the events too literally. He is the epitome of literalness and earnestness and quite the maddest character in the play, never further from the truth than when he's congratulating himself on having found the right answers. He is certainly right when he tells Prentice,

> You can't be a rationalist in an irrational world. It isn't rational.

But he is the one who creates the unreason. Nothing is real to him till it's been turned into a theory. He can't really see facts at all: when people press them on him, he converts them at lightning speed into monstrous theses, as when Geraldine, weary of her boy disguise, says, "I can't go on, doctor! . . . I'm not a boy! I'm a girl!" and he snaps it up, "Excellent. A confession at last. He wishes to believe he's a girl in order to minimize the feelings of guilt he experiences after homosexual intercourse." Or when Prentice recklessly ventures a joke about white golliwogs—"She's making white golliwogs for sale in colour prejudice trouble-spots"—only to have it drawn into the humourless Rance analysis—"What was the object in creating these nightmare creatures? . . . The man's a second Frankenstein."

Earnestness is the root vice of the play: all the other ills are seen branching out from it, above all the determination to categorize and label and pin people down that afflicts characters in this play as it does, though in so much more mild and decorous forms, in *The Importance of Being Earnest*. The comparison with Wilde can hardly be avoided—even his title would be appropriate to Orton's play, the resemblances of plot and theme are so striking. It wouldn't be so true to the tone, however. Orton's title, *What the Butler Saw*, exactly catches the saucy and slightly menacing notes, its bold, highly coloured quality.

The features of his style which are indicated by this splendidly right title are also the features which relate Orton to the modern movement in the English theatre and make him one of the chief influences in it. Farce is, as Eric Bentley says, the most direct of forms, but even within the convention Orton's is remarkable for the directness of its impact. Comparisons with Wilde—or Pinero, or for that matter Sardou and the French farceurs—bring out how much more thoroughly and ruthlessly Orton involves us in the confusion of his characters. We are made dizzy like them by the bewildering sexual double bluffs, are scarcely sure at some points whether we're confronted with a girl dressed as a boy who is being taken for a boy who thinks himself a girl—or vice versa.

There's one such disorientating moment when Rance says to Nick in his girl's disguise—"Suppose I made an indecent suggestion to you? If you agreed something might occur which, by and large, would be regarded as natural. If, on the other hand, I approached this child—(He smiles at Geraldine)—my action could result only in a gross violation of the order of things." We surely begin to lose our hold on what *is* the natural order of things at this point, an effect Orton is evidently aiming at—he made this point explicitly in speaking of *Entertaining Mr. Sloane*: "What I wanted to do was break down all the sexual compartments people have."[4]

We experience too, I think—and this is very unexpected and surprising—a faint sense of poignancy as the chase works up to its desperate climax. No break with the farcical convention is involved in this. Rance is ludicrously wrong as usual when he lectures Dr. Prentice on his supposed bisexual tendencies: "There are two sexes. The unpalatable truth must be faced. Your attempts at a merger can end only in disaster." And yet his phrases catch the note of real desire that can occasionally be sensed behind the fantastic distortions, a real

[4]Interview, op. cit.

longing for the alluring, hermaphroditic wraith that has been created out of the hopeless confusion between Gerald and Geraldine.

This double effect is an impressive indication of Orton's maturing virtuosity. It rises so naturally out of the comic confusion, which depends on the action being taken at a dazzlingly fast speed. Speed is always the essence of farce but Orton's is the supersonic variety. He spends no time at all on preliminaries but goes straight to business with the directness of Dr. Prentice setting about his seduction of Geraldine. One sometimes wonders, indeed, if the mechanism isn't too fast, too loaded with repartee and fantastic turns of invention for slow, waking brains to take in. Orton seems to be aware of this danger; he deals with it by offering moments of rest, pauses for recapitulation and getting bearings. One such occurs towards the end when Dr. Prentice, Geraldine and Nick are left alone together while Rance, convinced now that they are all mad, goes off in search of tranquillizers.

> *Geraldine* (with a sob). Twice declared insane in one day! And they said I'd be working for a cheerful, well-spoken crowd. (She blows her nose.)
>
> *Nick.* Why is he wearing my uniform?
>
> *Prentice.* He isn't a boy. He's a girl.
>
> *Geraldine.* Why is she wearing my shoes?
>
> *Prentice.* She isn't a girl. She's a boy. (Pouring whisky.) Oh, if I live to be ninety, I'll never again attempt sexual intercourse.
>
> *Nick.* If we changed clothes, sir, we could get things back to normal.
>
> *Prentice.* We'd then have to account for the disappearance of my secretary and the page-boy.
>
> *Geraldine.* But they don't exist!
>
> *Prentice.* When people who don't exist disappear the account of their departure must be convincing.

Sanity momentarily returns here, or at any rate the nearest thing one can get to it in this situation of mad unreason. As Prentice says, "I've been too long among the mad to know what sanity is." But for a moment we're on relatively solid ground, we get a glimpse of a normal perspective before the chase starts off again and we hurtle on to the gorgeous confrontation between the two psychiatrists, one brandishing a gun, the other a strait jacket—"I'm going to certify you." I am going to certify you"—and the breathtaking climax when Prentice presses the alarm and chaos breaks out all over—a siren wails, grilles come down over the doors, the light goes out. For an unnerving instant we share the characters' panic: "An overloading of the circuit! We're trapped!" The thought of being shut up in Dr. Prentice's clinic for ever—or even for another five minutes—is enough to cause a shiver or two: the strait jacket and the padded cell have a rather horrid reality, after all.

Happily, Orton is able to get us right out of the dream in this play. A ladder descends, Sergeant Match appears as *deus ex machina,* a Bacchanalian bisexual god in a leopard-spotted dress torn from one shoulder and streaming with blood. "We're approaching what our racier novelists term 'the climax,'" says Rance in the ebullient spirit induced by the discovery that *all* his theories have been proved right and his thesis is well set for a runaway success ("Double incest is even more likely to produce a best-seller than murder"). The characters scamper through the remaining "explanations" and then "bleeding, drugged and drunk, climb the rope ladder into the blazing light."

"Let us put our clothes on and face the world." What resilience, and what a tonic experience to share in it! It seems especially poignant that Orton should have died as he did before this most freeing of his plays was produced, fallen into the brutal reality it lifts us so triumphantly out of. He manages in his farce to give us both a great id-releasing experience and a reassuring demonstration of the power of wit to control it: it's certainly reassuring to have all the mad earnestness of *What the Butler Saw* taken up into gaiety. Already it's clear (as I suggested in speaking of the realistic drama) that his drama has been a very influential model and it seems likely that he will continue to exert considerable influence through the playwrights who have assimilated elements of his style.

Tomfoolery:
Stoppard's Theatrical Puns

by Hersh Zeifman

Fasten your seat belts—the central character of Tom Stoppard's *Travesties*, a former British consular official in Zurich named Henry Carr, is about to take off on a wild ghostchase, racing through his memoirs with the aid of a faulty rear-view mirror and a horn which he blows only for himself, the throttle set breathlessly at full speed back and no breaks to speak of:

> What was he like, James Joyce, I am often asked. It is true that I knew him well at the height of his powers, his genius in full flood in the making of *Ulysses,* before publication and fame turned him into a public monument for pilgrim cameras more often than not in a velvet smoking jacket of an unknown colour, photography being in those days a black and white affair, but probably real blue if not empirical purple and sniffing a bunch of sultry violets that positively defy development. . . . Further recollections of a Consular Official in Whitest Switzerland. The Ups and Downs of Consular life in Zurich During the Great War: A Sketch. 'Twas in the bustling metropolis of swiftly gliding trams and greystone banking houses, of cosmopolitan restaurants on the great stone banks of the swiftly-gliding snot-green (mucus mutandis) Limmat River, of jewelled escapements and refugees of all kinds, e.g. Lenin. . . .

Travesties is Stoppard at his most verbally dazzling, and the above passage is fairly typical of the play as a whole: brim-full

"Tomfoolery: Stoppard's Theatrical Puns." From Hersh Zeifman. "Tomfoolery: Stoppard's Theatrical Puns," *The Yearbook of English Studies,* ix(1979), pp. 204–20. Copyright © 1979 by the Modern Humanities Research Association. Reprinted by permission of the Editors.

(some might say overflowing) with puns of all manner and description, ranging from the ridiculous to the sublime, from the groaningly obvious to the diabolically subtle. And however many one thinks one has detected, there are always others somewhere in the shadows; rereading a Stoppard text means constantly being startled by fresh discoveries.

Puns are both the glory and the bane of Stoppard's critical reputation. On the one hand, his plays are feasts of language; in a time of almost universal famine, it is hardly surprising that audiences have gratefully responded by gorging themselves into paroxysms of delight. The exuberance and inventiveness of Stoppard's puns are difficult to resist, so seductive are they and so starved are we for any kind of verbal elegance in the theatre. On the other hand, there are those "virtuous" few who wish to abolish theatrical cakes and ale. The truly hostile critics seem to regard punning itself, whatever the merits of any particular pun, as essentially sophomoric: a vaguely shameful adolescent activity that, if indulged in overmuch, results in blindness or insanity. Slightly more sympathetic critics, those who damn Stoppard with faint praise, may acknowledge, if backed into a corner and threatened with unspeakable torture, that his puns are indeed witty and clever, but, oh dear, *merely* clever, too clever by half.

Both of these critical responses seem to me to be almost wilfully blinkered, in that they refuse to look at Stoppard's puns in their wider dramatic context. Stoppard is clearly obsessed with puns, and, like Coward before him, he has an undeniable "talent to amuse." But although amusement for its own sake is an honourable theatrical intention hardly deserving the scorn and abuse we sometimes snobbishly and stupidly heap on it, Stoppard's puns are there not only to amuse. Amuse they certainly do, and amuse they were intended to do, but they have other functions as well. Stoppard uses puns, carefully and deliberately, as structural devices in his plays, as an integral part of the play's basic "meaning." Just as form invariably mirrors content in Stoppard's drama (indeed, form frequently *becomes* content), so too do patterns of language, and particularly puns.

In *Rosencrantz and Guildenstern Are Dead,* Stoppard's first

major critical success, the two shadowy courtiers on the
fringes of *Hamlet* consider at one point the precise implications of Claudius's promise to reward them handsomely for
helping to determine the cause of Hamlet's unhappiness:

> *Guil.* And receive such thanks as fits a king's remembrance.
> *Ros.* I like the sound of that. What do you think he means by
>   remembrance?
> *Guil.* He doesn't forget his friends.
> *Ros.* Would you care to estimate?
> *Guil.* Difficult to say, really—some kings tend to be amnesiac,
>   others I suppose the opposite, whatever that is . . .
> *Ros.* Yes—but—
> *Guil.* Elephantine . . . ?
> *Ros.* Not how long—how much?
> *Guil.* *Retentive*—he's a very retentive king, a royal retainer . . .

Guildenstern is the first in Stoppard's long line of compulsive
punsters, and we laugh at the agility of his mind and the
nimbleness of his wit: he is having fun with language, playing
with it, and we share his pleasure. But the passage continues:

> *Ros.* What are you playing at?
> *Guil.* Words, words. They're all we have to go on.

Suddenly, the joking becomes "darker," more sinister. For
Rosencrantz and Guildenstern are living out the actor's traditional nightmare with a vengeance; thrust on to the stage, they
are forced to take part in a play of which they are totally
ignorant, their lines not simply forgotten but never learned.
Their response is, not surprisingly, panic, but it is panic of a
specifically metaphysical kind, for it quickly becomes clear
that what Stoppard is offering us here is a metaphor of life.
   The play-life metaphor is greatly facilitated by the truly
astonishing range of puns linking the two concepts ("We don't
know how to *act*"; "We are entitled to some direction"; etc.).
Comparing life to a play may well be the hoariest of theatrical
clichés, but Stoppard manages to make it seem fresh through
an audacious and dazzling use of *Hamlet*. Like Rosencrantz
and Guildenstern, we too are actors in a play, our life, which,
like *Hamlet*, is in one sense a tragedy, in that it inevitably ends
with our death, but in another sense is also a kind of farce. For

we are not even given the dignity of being the main characters, of occupying centre stage. Life is like the play *Hamlet*, and we find ourselves cast as Rosencrantz and Guildenstern, secondary characters who are expendable in more ways than one (many productions of *Hamlet* omit them entirely), insignificant little ciphers who never really understand what is going on. And there is the crux of the issue: the play of our life proceeds bewilderingly around us, as *Hamlet* does around Ros and Guil, and, like them, we try desperately to pick up our cues, to muddle through it somehow, even though we have no idea of the plot, our place in the action, our motivations, the *purpose* of it all. "What in God's name is going on?" Guildenstern cries out, but, needless to say, nobody answers. Is it possible to answer? Life is a terrible riddle, an enigma; and what better way to reflect this metaphysical riddle than through a series of linguistic riddles, a series of puns.

The opening image of *Rosencrantz and Guildenstern Are Dead* is of two men spinning coins; but at the same time, in an equivalent verbal image, it is also words that are being spun. The most common form of pun in the play is precisely this spinning of words: a single sound is seen to possess more than a single meaning:

> *Guil. (musing).* The law of probability, it has been oddly asserted, is something to do with the proposition that if six monkeys *(he has surprised himself)* . . . if six monkeys were . . .
> *Ros.* Game?
> *Guil.* Were they?
> *Ros.* Are you?
> *Guil. (understanding).* Game. *(Flips a coin.)*

Rosencrantz means by "game" one thing, Guildenstern another. Like a coin, this type of pun lands sometimes on heads (meaning A), sometimes on tails (meaning B), sometimes on its edge (meaning C), and, most frightening of all, sometimes disappears altogether, as though the sheer multiplicity of meanings had caused it to implode.[1] The result is linguistic confusion; the same word or phrase may mean any

[1]In Act II of the play, Rosencrantz performs a coin trick in which the coin actually does disappear, much to his amazement: "*Ros stops laughing, looks around his feet, pats his clothes, puzzled.*"

number of things. "Are we all right for England?," Rosencrantz enquires of the Player when they meet on the boat: meaning, are they headed in the right direction? "You look all right to me. I don't think they're very particular in England," replies the Player. There are countless examples of this sort of pun in *Rosencrantz and Guildenstern Are Dead*. Words may indeed be all we have to go on, but in Stoppard's plays words are, more often than not, puns: ambiguous, confusing, enigmatic. For the reality those puns reflect is itself enigmatic. The spinning of words thus becomes a symbol for the spinning of webs; linguistic uncertainty mirrors metaphysical uncertainty. And we are trapped in those webs, in a world in which there is such a confusing multiplicity of possible meaning that the whole concept of meaning ultimately becomes meaningless.

The pervasiveness of puns in the play extends, by analogy, to the title-characters themselves. One of the play's comic leitmotifs is the confusion that constantly arises over which of them is Rosencrantz and which is Guildenstern, a confusion which they themselves share. This identity mix-up is amusing, but it is also terrifying. For the two characters are not, in terms of their personalities, interchangeable, as Guil, at least, is painfully aware (indeed, the fact that he is aware is itself a sign of their difference: Guil is generally much brighter than Ros). And yet, in terms of their "fate," they may as well be one person: for the purposes of *Hamlet*, Ros and Guil *are* interchangeable. In effect, then, Ros and Guil have become a kind of pun: two separate and distinct "identities" happening to share a single unit (Rosencrantzandguildenstern), just as, in a linguistic pun, two separate and distinct meanings happen to share a single sound. And, as with all puns, the inevitable result is confusion: human identity is as puzzling as linguistic identity.

Underlying this problem of metaphysical uncertainty is a more basic problem in epistemology. As George Moore, the philosopher in *Jumpers* who spends the entire play attempting to prove through logical inference the existence of God, muses at one point: "How does one know what it is one believes when it's so difficult to know what it is one knows." In Stoppard's one-act play *After Magritte*, Harris claims he *knows* that the mysterious figure hopping down the street was a

blind, one-legged, white-bearded gentleman wearing striped
pyjamas, carrying a turtle under one arm, and brandishing a
white stick, because he *saw* him ("I happened to see him with
my own eyes"). "We all saw him" is his wife Thelma's unan-
swerable comeback, and yet her description of the figure is
totally at odds with that of her husband. This is merely one of
the play's three visual puzzles designed to dramatize the fact
that appearances can be deceptive: what we *think* we "see" may
not be the "truth" at all.

The first visual puzzle is the play's opening tableau, the
utter lunacy of which may be grasped from a description of
just one of the play's characters:

> *Mother is lying on her back on the ironing board, her head to Stage R, her*
> *downstage foot up against the flat of the iron. A white bath towel covers her*
> *from ankle to chin. Her head and part of her face are concealed in a*
> *tight-fitting black rubber bathing cap. A black bowler hat reposes on her*
> *stomach. She could be dead; but is not.*

The stage picture seems, at first glance, surrealistic, like a
painting by Magritte.[2] Hence the pun concealed in the play's
title. Ostensibly, the title refers to the chronological time of the
play's action: we first meet the Harris family "after Magritte":
that is, after they have returned from viewing the Magritte
exhibition at the Tate. But the whole play is like a Magritte
painting: that is, it is "after Magritte" *stylistically*, in the sense of
"in the manner of Magritte." Stoppard has not, in fact, written
a truly surrealist play, but, like the surrealists, he too is dedi-
cated to revising our sense of reality, questioning our perception of "truth."

The initial tableau may indeed appear bizarre and mean-

---

[2]Compare, for example, Magritte's *L'assassin menacé* (1926), which has
much the same kind of "surreal" quality as the opening tableau in *After
Magritte*. In the painting, a man is seen listening to a gramophone (the horn
of which is like an Ur-tuba), while a naked woman (or possibly a manne-
quin), whom he has presumably just killed, lies on a nearby sofa, bleeding
from her mouth. Spying on this bizarre scene from a window outside are
three figures, of whom we see only their faces and upper torsos (like
Holmes, in Stoppard's play, who *"might be a cut-out figure; but is not"*). Two
bowler-hatted detectives, armed with bludgeon and net, stand on either side
of the doorway, ready to pounce. Eerily, all the figures in the painting seem
to have the identical face.

ingless, but Stoppard gradually feeds us enough information
to force us to change our opinion: the seemingly "illogical" has
a perfectly logical explanation. By the time we reach the play's
final visual puzzle, the shift in our perspective is complete. To
the uninitiated (like the policeman Holmes, who recoils in
stunned horror), the closing tableau looks as insane as the
opening tableau once did to *our* eyes. But we have been made
to understand in the interim how the apparently irrefutable
evidence of our senses can frequently be misleading. "Seeing
is believing" may be a catchy maxim, but what happens when
the whole question of precisely what it is that we "see" has been
placed in doubt?

This issue of the unreliability of our senses, the slippery
elusiveness of empirical "truth," is underscored by Stoppard's
use of puns in the play. For language may be equally elusive,
equally ambiguous. The very first words spoken in *After Magritte* provide an excellent illustration of this point. Harris, as
part of the seemingly grotesque opening tableau, is seen
standing on a chair, blowing into the lampshade suspended
over his head:

> *Thelma.* It's electric, dear.
> *Harris (mildly).* I didn't think it was a flaming torch.
> *Thelma.* There's no need to use language. That's what I always
> say.

Harris uses the word "flaming" literally (that is, "I didn't think
it was a fire-torch"); his wife thinks he is using it as a mild
obscenity. Although Thelma means by "language" specifically
"*bad* language," she is ironically right on the most literal level:
there is in fact no need to use *language* because the same point
has already been made *visually*. Remember the description of
Mother in that opening tableau: "*She could be dead; but is not.*"
Similarly, Harris could be swearing; but is not.[3] The use of

---

[3]Stoppard makes this equation explicit in the stage direction of a
slightly later episode:

> *(There is a piercing scream, from Mother, as she jerks her foot away from the
> heated-up iron ... Her first audible word seems to be a vulgarity; but is not.)*
> *Mother.* Butter!
> *Thelma (primly).* Now there's no need to use language—

puns thus merely parallels, on a verbal level, what is already implicit on a visual level: our "perceptions" may deceive us.

Having firmly set the tone in his opening dialogue, Stoppard proceeds to bombard us with a series of ever-more-outrageous puns, all designed to emphasize this central thematic issue. Language is as confusing and difficult to interpret as are visual signs. Sometimes the pun results from homophones:

> *Harris.* The most—*the very most*—I am prepared to concede is that
> he *may* have been a sort of street arab making off with his
> lute . . .
> *Thelma.* His *loot?*
> *Harris (expansively).* Or his mandolin—Who's to say?

And sometimes it stems from the same word having more than one meaning or association, a pun which, when added to the homophone (or near-homophone) pun, creates double confusion. In the following dialogue, for example, Detective Inspector Foot, under the mistaken impression that Mother is a deranged surgeon, misinterprets her innocent request to be allowed to play the tuba:

> *Mother.* Is it all right for me to practice?
> *Foot.* No, it is not all right! Ministry standards may be lax but we
> draw the line at Home Surgery to bring in the little luxuries of
> life.
> *Mother.* I only practice on the tuba.
> *Foot.* Tuba, femur, fibula—it takes more than a penchant for
> rubber gloves to get a license nowadays.

Stoppard's radio play *Artist Descending a Staircase* continues his attack on our perception of "truth" by extending the argument to include sound as well as sight. On at least one level, then, *Artist* is a kind of aural version of *After Magritte,* its title likewise encapsulating the play's theme by means of a buried pun. Marcel Duchamp's cubist masterpiece *Nude Descending a Staircase* (1911–12) was originally greeted with scorn and outrage: why give a specifically representational title to a mere blob of cubist shapes? Where was the nude, or the descent, or the staircase? If such questions now appear faintly ludicrous, it is because we have learned to "see" differently.

Duchamp had indeed painted a nude descending a staircase, but a shift in our perception was required before we could understand the real significance of the title. Similarly, Stoppard's play is indeed about an artist descending a staircase (literally, fatally) but a shift in our perception is required before we can understand the significance of *that* title (it is not a "descent" in the way we at first assume). Just as what we *think* we "see" is ambiguous and may not represent the "truth" at all, so what we think we "hear" is equally problematic.

The play opens with two artists, Beauchamp and Martello, listening to a tape recording which has inadvertently recorded the final moments of life of their friend and fellow-artist Donner. The sounds on the tape appear to be unambiguous, and are interpreted by Beauchamp and Martello (and, of course, by us too, for, this being a radio play, we are in precisely the same position as they, that is, we also are restricted solely to listening) as follows:

(*a*) *Donner dozing: an irregular droning noise.*
(*b*) *Careful footsteps approach. The effect is stealthy. A board creaks.*
(*c*) *This wakes Donner, i.e. the droning stops in mid-beat.*
(*d*) *The footsteps freeze.*
(*e*) *Donner's voice, unalarmed: "Ah! There you are . . ."*
(*f*) *Two more quick steps, and then Thump!*
(*g*) *Donner cries out.*
(*h*) *Wood cracks as he falls through a balustrade.*
(*i*) *He falls heavily down the stairs, with a final sickening thump when he hits the bottom.*
   Silence.

Since Donner was obviously expecting his assailant ("*unalarmed: 'Ah! There you are . . .'* "), and since, as a semi-recluse, he had for years seen only Beauchamp and Martello, the single issue in dispute would appear to be which of them in fact murdered him. Each accuses the other, but one of them must be lying; as Martello so logically points out: "The tape recorder speaks for itself." Martello's statement is the aural equivalent of Harris's "I happened to see him with my own eyes." Hearing, like seeing, is believing; but can we ever be certain of exactly what it is that we have heard?

Stoppard is being particularly cunning in this play, set-

ting a fiendishly clever trap for us with great efficiency.
(There are no flies on Stoppard, although the same, alas,
cannot be said of Donner. The key to the trap is that the
"irregular droning noise" on the tape, which everyone interprets as the sound of "Donner dozing," is in fact the sound
made by a fly; or rather, it is almost certainly the sound made
by a fly, which is about as close to certainty as we shall ever get.
If we now return to the sequence of events on the tape,
bearing this correction in mind, our assumptions about how
Donner met his death will alter drastically.) Even more fiendishly clever, however, is that, at the same time as he is setting
this trap, Stoppard is also gleefully racing around warning us
that there *is* a trap—not that anyone takes any notice, of
course. It is rather like shouting "The telephone is ringing" to
a man who is stone deaf; if he could hear what you were
shouting, there would be no need for you to shout it, since he
would have heard the phone ringing in the first place. *Artist* is
filled with clues warning us that what we *think* we hear can be
deceptive, but naturally we do not hear them. The sound of a
buzzing fly, for example, occurs repeatedly in the play (Stoppard is teasing us mercilessly) but we never make the connection. And then there is the character of Sophie, who, being
blind, is forced to rely on her other senses. Although manag-
ing surprisingly well most of the time, Sophie, despite her
name, can still be fooled on occasion. Thus, on her first visit to
the artists' flat, she assumes, quite reasonably from what she
hears, that the men are engaged in a game of ping-pong. What
Sophie has in fact been hearing, however, is Beauchamp's
gramophone record of various games and pastimes. Sophie is
meant to stand as a warning to the audience, for we share her
dilemma: in a radio play we too are blind (literally in the dark),
we too must rely on our faculty of hearing, and we too are
constantly in danger of being misled.[4]

[4]There is also the possibility that Sophie has erred in visual perception,
as well. Thus, her attraction to Beauchamp is based on the premise that he
was the one who had painted what she describes as "a row of black stripes on
a white background" (she saw this painting before she became totally blind).
But was it really Beauchamp's painting (black railings on a field of snow) she
had in mind? Might it not have been Donner's (black gaps between the thick
white posts of a fence)? The entire Sophie–Beauchamp liaison may thus
have been founded on a misunderstanding.

Stoppard's use of puns in this play once again reinforces, structurally, the thematic point: characters constantly pick up on the wrong meaning of words, just as they constantly mis-hear the sounds around them. And, once again, the point is established in the very first lines of dialogue. The tape of Donner's death has been recorded on a continuous loop; when the sequence of sounds comes to an end, it begins all over again:

After a pause, this entire sequence begins again . . . Droning . . . Footsteps . . . (as before).
Martello. I think this is where I came in.
(Tape: "Ah! There you are . . .")
Beauchamp
And this is where you hit him.
(Tape: Thump!)

Beauchamp has interpreted Martello's comment as a confession of murder, whereas Martello was trying to signify only that the tape was starting to repeat itself ("I *mean*, it's going round again. The tape is going round in a *loop*"). And this kind of pun-confusion occurs repeatedly, and hilariously, in the text:

Martello. I will stand by you, Beauchamp. We have been together a long time.
Beauchamp. You may rely on me, Martello. I shall not cast the first stone. [i.e., speaking figuratively: I shall not condemn you]
Martello. You *have* cast it, Beauchamp [i.e., speaking literally: you have murdered Donner], but I do not prejudge you.
Beauchamp. My feelings precisely, but there seems to be some confusion in your mind—
Martello. My very thought. Turn off your machine, it seems to be disturbing your concentration—
(Tape: "Ah! —" and is switched off.)
Beauchamp. There you are. [meaning: I have turned it off]
Martello. On the contrary, Beauchamp, there *you* are. [meaning: that "Ah" on the tape was Donner's response to *your* arrival] Unless we can agree on *that,* I can't even begin to help you clear up this mess.
Beauchamp. Don't touch him, Martello.
Martello. I didn't mean clear up *Donner!*—honestly, Beauchamp, you buffoon!

The issue of epistemological uncertainty is further dramatized in *Jumpers*, and, as always in Stoppard, it is dramatized as much through form and structure as through content. Thus, it is not simply that the play's characters tell us that it is difficult to know anything for certain (although they repeatedly do); it is rather that we are made to experience this uncertainty directly. *Jumpers* consists of a bewildering series of events which we witness with our own eyes, yet the "truth" of which remains obstinately ambiguous. George Moore, the play's central character, suspects, for example, that his wife Dotty is having an affair with Archie, the Vice-Chancellor of the University at which George is Professor of Ethics. Dotty claims, on the other hand, that Archie (who is also a psychiatrist) is merely treating her medically. Which of them is right?

It certainly *appears* as if Archie and Dotty are sexually involved; but then, as we should surely realize by now, appearances can be deceptive, a fact which George himself acknowledges:

> *George.* Meeting a friend in a corridor, Wittgenstein said: "Tell me, why do people always say it was *natural* for men to assume that the sun went round the earth rather than that the earth was rotating?" His friend said, "Well, obviously, because it just *looks* as if the sun is going round the earth." To which the philosopher replied, "Well, what would it have looked like if it looked as if the earth was rotating?"

Still, when George enters Dotty's boudoir unexpectedly, and discovers Dotty and Archie in what seems to be a compromising position, he immediately assumes the worst:

> *Archie (through screen).* Relax, my dear!—Now over on your back—
> *George.* You must think I'm a bloody fool—
> *Archie.* What do you mean?
> *George.* Well, everything you do makes it *look* as if you're . . . (*Pause.*)
> *Archie.* Well, what would it have *looked* like if it had *looked* as if I were examining her?

George is stumped, and so are we: every single event we witness on the stage, no matter how straightforward it at first appears, is in fact shown to be rife with ambiguity.

Not surprisingly, this ambiguity is also reflected through Stoppard's usual vast array of puns. The certainty that we understand another's words proves to be as elusive as every other kind of certainty. Thus, while George is busy in his study trying to prove that God exists, Dotty is trapped in the bedroom with a dead body on her hands:

> *Dotty (off. Panic).* Help! Murder!
> *(George throws his manuscript on to the desk and marches angrily to the door.)*
> *(Off.)* Oh, horror, horror, horror! Confusion now hath made its masterpiece . . . most sacrilegious murder!—*(Different voice.)* Woe, alas! What, in our house?

George is annoyed because he interprets Dotty's cry "Murder!" figuratively, as one of her game-tactics designed to get him to stop working and pay her some attention, the equivalent of her crying wolf ("Dorothy, I will not have my work interrupted by these gratuitous acts of lupine delinquency!") But Dotty's cry, on the contrary, is horribly literal: there *has* been a murder. (And her quotes from *Macbeth* alluding to the slaying of King Duncan are not nearly so "whimsical" as they might at first appear; for the dead body in Dotty's boudoir is *Duncan* McFee, and he was killed in their house.) In point of fact, Dotty's tortured mind is mourning *three* murders, linked together in the text through a complex pattern of words and images: McFee; the astronaut abandoned on the moon; and God.

Puns resulting in this kind of confusion abound in *Jumpers*. "Play with me . . . ," Dotty implores George at one point. Interpreting "play" sexually, George hesitates: "Now . . . ?" "I mean *games*—," Dotty explains. Or consider the interchange in which Inspector Bones, convinced that Dotty has killed McFee, begins interrogating his suspect:

> *Bones.* Miss Moore, is there anything you wish to say at this stage?
> *Dotty (in the sense of "Pardon?").* Sorry?
> *Bones.* My dear, we are all *sorry*—

Jumpers ultimately circles back to the central concern of *Rosencrantz and Guildenstern Are Dead,* by relating the concept of epistemological confusion specifically to that of metaphysical confusion. There are two linked "mysteries" at the heart of

Jumpers: (a) Who killed Duncan McFee?; and (b) Does God exist? George thinks that he knows the answer to both questions. By "examin[ing] the data" and "look[ing] for logical inferences," George feels he can prove the existence of God, in the same way that he is convinced that "poor" Dotty killed McFee, "as sure as she killed my poor Thumper." But poor Dotty almost certainly did *not* kill poor Thumper, George's pet hare: poor George killed him. (At any rate, it *appears* to have been George.)[5] How valid, then, are the rest of George's "certainties"? It is impossible to say, and that of course is the point: the data are simply too ambiguous, too misleading. It is not that the mysteries do not have solutions (after all, God either exists or He does not); it is, rather, that we are unable to discover those solutions. As Archie points out: "Unlike mystery novels, life does not guarantee a dénouement; and if it came, how would one know whether to believe it?" Thus, despite having seen McFee murdered in front of our eyes, we can never *know* who killed him (half the play's characters had both motive and opportunity). And what applies to the physical applies even more strongly to the metaphysical: by the same token, therefore, we can never really *know* that God exists. The basic "truths" of existence are shrouded in mystery; in any case, how can we hope to discover those "truths" when our very means of discovery are themselves highly suspect?

The most one can do is cling to a kind of blind, stubborn

[5]Since Thumper is later discovered impaled on an arrow in George's wardrobe, he was presumably killed when George, startled by Dotty's yelling "Fire!," blindly shot his arrow into the wardrobe. And yet, Dotty did yell "Fire!," even though she meant "conflagration," even though she meant it metaphorically: could she then be considered, in a sense, to have indeed murdered Thumper? Or maybe Thumper was already dead, killed by a different arrow. That way, of course, madness lies; or, at the very least, a severe headache. Still, so wary does the play make us of trusting the evidence of our senses that we find ourselves fighting in this way against "certainty," even in the case of the one "murder" which seems absolutely iron-clad: George's stepping on his pet tortoise. Despite our actually seeing this happen, and hearing the fatal "CRRRRRUNCH!!!," we search wildly for other possible explanations: perhaps the tortoise died of a heart attack, say. (Shell shock?)

faith; what it finally comes down to, then, is not logic but magic:

> *George.* Yes, I'm something of a logician . . .
> *Bones.* Really? Sawing ladies in half, that sort of thing?
> *George. Lo*gician.

Bones's unwitting pun is closer to the truth than George realizes. George has spent the entire play refusing to be a "Jumper" ("I belong to a school which regards all sudden movements as ill-bred"), refusing, that is, to join the University gymnastic team headed by Archie, to jump on Archie's Rad-Lib bandwagon, to exchange his deeply held moral convictions for a philosophy with more "bounce," a philosophy that glorifies pragmatism and expediency. He refuses, in other words, to *become* Archie (or, as he is more formally known, Sir Archibald *Jumper*,[6] M.D., D.Phil., D.Litt., L.D., D.P.M., D.P.T. (Gym)). Yet, ironically, George does wind up being a "Jumper," in still another sense of that multi-layered pun: he makes a "leap" into faith. George's God, like all metaphysical "certainties," is pulled out of his hat rather than his head: produced, not by the thoughtwaves of a logical mind, but by the handwaves of a magical wand.

And yet, despite George's being terribly muddled and ineffectual, our sympathies go with him. For the opposition in this debate on God and morality, Archie's Rad-Lib philosophy, is presented as somehow corrupt and callous. Part of this effect is achieved through the Rad-Libs' use of puns: their approach to language is to stretch it unmercifully on the rack, to make language accommodate, and so give respectability to, a debased reality. Look at Dotty, for example, desperately trying, through language, to make sense of that which makes no sense:

> *George.* Are you telling me that the Radical Liberal spokesman for Agriculture has been made Archbishop of Canterbury?!!

---

[6]Like a number of other Stoppard characters (for example, Ispector Bones's osteopath brother), Archie suffers from the "Cognomen Syndrome."

Dotty.   Don't shout at *me* . . . I suppose if you think of him as a sort
    of . . . shepherd, ministering to his flock . . .

The above example is amusing enough, but it also has its
uglier side. Thus Archie, through a truly hideous pun, indicates his pragmatic indifference to the death of the astronaut
abandoned on the moon:

> Captain Scott . . . I should like you to imagine if you will the scene
> of events last Thursday morning, the main point and feature
> being that it was a planet entirely uninhabited, was it not, save for
> yourself and Captain Oates. You have lately returned from there.
> Your friend, Captain Oates, has not, and must be presumed late.

While we may sympathize with George's point of view,
however, he is engaged in a debate which nobody can be said
to "win." The structure of *Jumpers,* like the structure of most of
Stoppard's plays, is essentially dialectical, but without a final
synthesis ever being reached. Stoppard has himself drawn
attention to this aspect of his plays:

> The element which I find most valuable [in my work] is the one
> that other people are put off by—that is, that there is very often
> *no* single, clear statement in my plays. What there is, is a series
> of conflicting statements made by conflicting characters, and
> they tend to play a sort of infinite leap-frog. You know, an
> argument, a refutation, then a rebuttal of the refutation, then a
> counter-rebuttal, so that there is never any point in this intel-
> lectual leap-frog at which I feel *that* is the speech to stop it on,
> *that* is the last word.[7]

The "endless debate" format of his plays, in terms of both
their content and their form, reflects Stoppard's own intellectual searching, his uncertainty about the "right" answer. In his
novel *Lord Malquist and Mr. Moon,* there is a scene in which the
hero Moon finds himself spinning round so quickly that he
becomes dizzy and falls backwards into a bath filled with
water:

[7]"Ambushes for the Audience: Towards a High Comedy of Ideas,"
Interview with Stoppard, *Theatre Quarterly,* 4, No. 14 (May–July 1974), 3–17
(pp. 6–7).

"I got dizzy," he explained.

"I should think you did—what were you *doing*?"

"Nothing," said Moon. "I was trying to face one way or the other, and I got confused and fell over."

Let that be my epitaph.

Who is the speaker of that final, disembodied statement? On the one hand, it is Moon, schizophrenically both actor and narrator in this story. But it is also Stoppard, who, similarly schizophrenic, likewise gets dizzy from so constantly shifting position, from trying to see both sides of an issue at once. What we are in fact witnessing in Stoppard's drama, then, is a theatricalization, an externalization, of his own internal debates. The argument split among various characters on a stage is really Stoppard arguing with himself ("I write plays," he has commented, "because dialogue is the most respectable way of contradicting myself").[8]

Puns are a perfect way of conveying, through language, this dialectical structure of Stoppard's drama. For nothing is more schizophrenic, by definition, than a pun: two or more utterly different meanings are yoked violently together in the strait-jacket of a single word (or two words that sound alike). It is language arguing with itself. And all that is required to set the dialectical ball really rolling is for one character to assume meaning A while another character opts for meaning B. A pun is thus quintessentially dialectical, containing within itself its own thesis and antithesis. On occasion, some of Stoppard's characters make deliberate use of this "doubleness" of puns, attacking their opponents in a series of punnic wars which can be fought with relative impunity. It is a deliciously funny and effective form of aggression, at one and the same time ostensibly inoffensive and yet teasingly (or viciously) hostile.

In *Artist Descending a Staircase*, for example, Martello has a go at Donner's outrageous concept of edible art, represented by a statue made of sugar ("It will give cubism a new lease of life," Martello notes sweetly). And sugar is only the beginning:

[8]Jon Bradshaw, "Tom Stoppard, Nonstop Word Games With a Hit Playwright," *New York*, 10 January 1977, 47–51 (p. 51).

Martello. Your signed loaves of bread reproduced in sculpted
dough, *baked* . . . your ceramic steaks carved from meat! It will
give opinion back to the intellectuals and put taste where it
belongs. From now on the artist's palate—
Donner. Are you laughing at me, Martello?
Martello. Certainly not, Donner. Let them eat art.

Along the same lines but far less teasing is Tzara's "confused"
response to Joyce's poetry in *Travesties*:

Tzara (to Joyce). For your masterpiece I have great expectorations
    (Gwen's squeak, "Oh!")
    For you I would eructate a monument.
    (Oh!)
    Art for art's sake—I defecate!
Gwen. Delectate . . .
Tzara. I'm a foreigner.

But Stoppard's characters do not need to use *deliberate*
puns in order to indicate their opposition to each other. For
even when they do not appear to be arguing, the "inadver-
tent" puns they constantly employ give clear evidence of the
wide gulf that inevitably separates them. The debate format in
Stoppard's drama is therefore as much a linguistic as a structural principle, implicit in the very use of puns itself. Illustra-
tions of this kind of basic linguistic opposition can be found in
all Stoppard's plays, but perhaps the classic example occurs in
Travesties. Thus, Cecily and Carr are poles apart politically and
artistically; Cecily is an ardent socialist and disciple of Lenin,
believing that the "sole duty and justification for art is social
criticism," whereas Carr is at the extreme other end of the
spectrum ("art doesn't change society, it is merely changed by
it"). In Act II they have an explicit and extremely heated
argument in which they defend their respective positions, but
the opposition between them is evident in far subtler ways, in
how they misunderstand each other's language, for example.
Here are the socialist Cecily and the aristocrat Carr discussing
the "servant problem":

Cecily. I am afraid that I disapprove of servants.
Carr. You are quite right to do so. Most of them are without
scruples.

Cecily. In the socialist future, no one will have any. [i.e., servants]
Carr. So I believe [i.e., scruples]

And here they are in the library, where Cecily spends her spare time helping Lenin research his book on capitalism:

Cecily. I'm afraid I am too busy to reform you today. I must spend the lunch hour preparing references for Lenin.
Carr. Some faithful governess seeking fresh pastures?

It is like a conversation between two different species, each of whom inhabits a totally different world, speaks, in effect, almost literally a different language. There is thus no real need for Cecily and Carr to indicate their differences explicitly through verbal argument; their puns are already doing the job implicitly, and doing it extremely well.

Travesties, as indicated previously, is probably Stoppard's most sustained work of theatrical punning. Henry Carr is a punster's dream (or nightmare, depending on one's point of view); if language is a feast of words, then Carr arrives prepared with fork and knife in tongue, his double-edged and often cutting puns tumbling forth in an unstoppable flow. Some of his puns are outrageous ("What did it do in the Great War, Dada, I am often asked"); some ingeniously subtle ("who'd have thought big oaks from *a corn*er room at number 14 Spiegelgasse?" [my italics]); and some sneak up on us so quickly that we are too stunned even to try and categorize them:

Tzara. Eating and drinking, as usual, I see, Henry? I have often observed that Stoical principles are more easily borne by those of Epicurean habits.
Carr (stiffly). I believe it is done to drink a glass of hock and seltzer before luncheon, and it is well done to drink it well before luncheon. I took to drinking hock and seltzer for my nerves at a time when nerves were fashionable in good society. This season it is trenchfoot, but I drink it regardless because I feel much better after it.
Tzara. You might have felt much better anyway.
Carr. No, no—post hock, propter hock.

The cumulative effect of all these puns on an average audience is one of helpless, giddy laughter. But even in *Traves-*

ties, which comes the closest of Stoppard's major plays to using puns for their sheer verve and verbal wit, puns function as more than simply laugh-getters. Once again Stoppard is using puns structurally, to shape our response to the play's larger issues, although the issues have now shifted somewhat. In a recent interview, Ross Wetzsteon complimented Stoppard on the "fairness" with which he treated the various theories of art and revolution in *Travesties*:

> It seemed to me that one of the strengths of the play, one of the signs of [Stoppard's] maturity, was that he gave equal weight to Joyce, Lenin, and Tzara, that he allowed each of them to speak without choosing sides. Stoppard only partly agreed. "Equally *just,* I hope, but not equal weight. Of course I don't want to give any of them shallow arguments and then knock them down. No, you have to give the best possible argument to each of them. It's like playing chess with yourself—you have to try to win just as hard with black as you do with white. But while my sympathies may be divided in that sense, I find Joyce infinitely the most important."[9]

Stoppard weights the play in favour of Joyce through various structural stratagems. Thus, for example, Joyce is deliberately given the last word: literally, in his crucial argument with Tzara, and figuratively (and more subtly) at the close of each Act. Act I ends with Carr's devastating reminiscence: "I dreamed about [Joyce], dreamed I had him in the witness box, a masterly cross-examination, case practically won, admitted it all, the whole thing, the trousers, everything, and I *flung* at him— 'And what did you do in the Great War?' 'I wrote *Ulysses,*' he said. 'What did you do?' Bloody nerve"; while the final moments of Act II again remind us of *Ulysses* through Old Cecily's sly echo of Molly Bloom: "I do remember Joyce, yes you are quite right and he was Irish with glasses but that was the year after—1918—and the train had long gone from the station! I waved a red hanky and cried long live the revolution as the carriage took [Lenin] away in his bowler hat and yes, I said yes when you asked me. . . ."

[9]Ross Wetzsteon, "Tom Stoppard Eats Steak Tartare With Chocolate Sauce," *The Village Voice,* 10 November 1975, p. 121.

But perhaps the most effective (because the most insidious) structural stratagem nudging our sympathies towards Joyce is the sheer presence of all those marvellous puns in the play. The irony here is exquisite. Everything Carr says about Joyce is meant to ridicule and discredit the author of *Ulysses*; but the way in which Carr says it, the dazzling, exhilarating play with words, betrays his intentions, having precisely the opposite effect of vindicating Joyce in our eyes. It is not that, in the debate on art and revolution which lies at the centre of *Travesties*, Joyce is necessarily given the best lines: both Tzara and Lenin are allowed equal representation. Indeed, in terms of the actual substance of its argument, the outcome of the debate is left, typically for Stoppard, deliberately unresolved. But because we are so bowled over, so elated by Carr's dizzying sleight of words, we find ourselves, almost subliminally, identifying with Joyce, that quintessential punster and wordsmith.

Puns fly as fast and as furiously as ever in Stoppard's recent *Dirty Linen*. We have already seen in Stoppard's drama how puns can produce a genuine, "innocent" confusion; here we see that innocent confusion turned into deliberate duplicity. Each of the Members of Parliament whom we meet in the play has been sexually involved with Maddie Gotobed, although each of them is desperately trying to cover up that fact. Puns function in *Dirty Linen* as a kind of verbal equivalent of this attempt to keep the truth hidden, as a way of pulling the wool over people's ears. In the following passage, for example, McTeazle is trying to have a private conversation with Maddie, only to be constantly interrupted by Cocklebury-Smythe's flitting in and out of the room. The italicized words correspond to Cocklebury-Smythe's momentary reappearances; note how McTeazle is forced to shift into puns as a way of deceiving his colleague:

> *McTeazle.* Maddie*ning the way one is kept waiting for* ours is a very tricky position, my dear. In normal times one can count on chaps being quite sympathetic to the sight of a Member of Parliament having dinner with a lovely young woman in some out-of-the-way nook—it could be a case of constituency business, they're not necessarily screw–*oo–ooge is, I think you'll find, not in "David Copperfield" at all, still less in "The Old Curiosity Sho*

"—cking though it is, the sight of a Member of Parliament
having some out-of-the-way nookie with a lovely young woman
might well be a case of a genuine love match. . . .

What is funny here is not only the inventiveness of McTeazle's
mind, but the speed with which he is forced to extricate
himself, in sheer panic, from an embarrassing situation. (One
has really to sweat to transform, instantly, "screw" into Dick-
ens's "Scrooge,"and give it a believable context.)

Similarly, Withenshaw is likewise shown with his back to
the wall:

> You can't have a committee washing dirty linen in the corridors of
> power unless every member is above suspicion. *(On which he
> produces from the envelope a large pair of Y-front pants which he im-
> mediately shoves back into the envelope.)* The wheres and Y-fronts, the
> whys and wherefores of this Committee are clear to you all. Our
> presence here today is testimony to the trust the House has in us
> as individuals and that includes you Maddiemoiselle.

The "wheres and Y-fronts" pun, being so outrageous, is what
immediately grabs our attention. (This is not the only occasion, by the way, on which Withenshaw will be trapped by the
ubiquitous pair of briefs; later he will have to try and explain
their presence in his case by means of a truly desperate pun:
"It's a brief case.") But even funnier, because we know how
quickly and desperately his mind must be working, is the way
in which he glosses over his slip in knowing Maddie's first
name (he has claimed, at this point, never to have met her) by
transforming it into an "innocent" French gallantry ("Mad-
diemoiselle").

The more the Members of Parliament try to deceive their
colleagues, the more desperate their puns become, and the
more they keep giving themselves away. Thus Cocklebury-
Smythe, for example, becomes *"hysterical"* trying to mask his
clearly libidinous interest in Maddie:

> *(Cocklebury-Smythe has been standing like stone, his glazed eye ab-
> sently fixed on Maddie's cleavage.)*
> C-S. McTeazle, why don't you go and see if you can raise those
> great tits–boobs–those boobies, absolute tits, don't you agree,
> Malcolm and Douglas—though good men as well, of course,

useful chaps, very decent, first rate, two of the best, Malcolm
and Douglas, why don't you have a quick poke, peek, in the
Members' Bra—or the cafeteria, they're probably guzzling coffee and Swedish panties *(Maddie has crossed her legs)* Danish. . . .

The note of hysteria here emphasizes the fact that *Dirty Linen*
is, of course, a farce, and the use of puns is an excellent way of
mirroring, linguistically, what the farce form is doing structurally. For the earmarks of farce are lightning speed, mistaken identity, wild confusion, and, above all, a tone of barely
suppressed hysteria: a description which, though no coincidence, applies precisely to the nature of puns in this play.
Once again, Stoppard is requiring that his puns do double
duty: they are there for their amusement value, certainly, but
they also lead us into the very heart of his play's theme and
structure.

Thus the point about Stoppard's puns is that they are not
simply comic devices, although there is a marked tendency for
many critics to regard them solely in that light. (Hence the
"My, isn't he clever" school of response, whether that is meant
as compliment or disparagement.) They are clearly *partly*
comic devices, and on that very important level they succeed
brilliantly. Of course, some puns are weaker than others, and
some are very weak indeed; perhaps, too, there is occasionally
the danger of over-bombardment, of failing to judge when
enough is enough. But, in general, Stoppard controls his puns
with dazzling skill. They are meant to make us laugh, and we
do laugh, uproariously; and that is in itself a sufficiently
impressive accomplishment.

But what is even more impressive is the way Stoppard
uses his puns *both* as a comic device *and* as an integral part of
what his plays are trying to communicate. Theatrically, Stoppard's plays are remarkably all of a piece. In this respect, as in
so many others, they echo the plays of Samuel Beckett. (Beckett has had an enormous influence on Stoppard's drama, an
influence slyly acknowledged by Stoppard in a lovely pun in
the coda to *Jumpers*: "Wham, bam, thank you Sam.") Each
theatrical element of a Beckett play is "saying" the same thing;
one can thus pick up the play's "message" not only from the
words the characters are speaking ("content" in its most obvi-

ous form), but from the way those words are formulated, say, or the characters' gestures, or the setting, or the very shape of the play. Much the same thing is true of Stoppard; the dramatic "message" is bodied forth in every aspect of the play, as readily apparent in the *kinds* of words his characters speak (for example, puns) as in the words themselves. And as the nature of that message shifts from play to play, so the specific implications of what punning can signify (because its range is extremely wide) likewise shift, so as to accommodate the new thematic concern. By thus being an intrinsic part of his plays' very fabric, rather than simply dramatic ornamentation appliqued on some wholly different fabric, Stoppard's puns may be said to constitute a truly theatrical language, in that their presence encapsulates, in a very real sense, the essence of what his plays are all about. Or, to switch the metaphor and end on a suitably outrageous punning note: in Stoppard's drama, punnology recapitulates ontology.

Victims of Circumstance:
Alan Ayckbourn's Plays

by Guido Almansi

"Someone who shall be nameless . . .": the phrase catches that middle-class philistinism which Alan Ayckbourn's prose so lovingly and sarcastically explores—Penelope Keith uttered it with proper priggishness of feature and voice in the recent television production of *Living Together*. In his plays such periphrases are followed by unequivocal comments concerning unwashed dishes or unemptied ashtrays. I suspect that *someone* who shall be nameless must have spoilt our pleasure and our capacity to think critically about humour, otherwise we would have already become aware of the presence of Ayckbourn as a seriously humorous writer. Humorous and serious: the two adjectives go together, in spite of what your Leavisite Sixth Form Master may have taught you. The invasion of Ayckbourniana in between Shaftesbury Avenue and the South Bank, the massive taking over of TV peak time last autumn and the recent publication of two books, *Three Plays* and *The Norman Conquests*,[1] ought to have induced even the most solemn theatre critic to take his farces very seriously indeed.

A good writer can afford and endure all sorts of human shortcomings: he can be slow-witted, unperceptive, ideologically muddled, psychologically obtuse—names and addresses

"Victims of Circumstance: Alan Ayckbourn's Plays." From Guido Almansi, "Victims of Circumstance: Alan Ayckbourn's Plays," *Encounter* (April, 1978), pp. 58–65. Copyright © 1978 by *Encounter*. Reprinted by permission of the author and Margaret Ramsay Ltd.

[1]*Three Plays. The Norman Conquests.* By Alan Ayckbourn. Chatto & Windus [London, 1977].

only for *bona fide* scholars. He can also be humourless, long-
winded and sentimentally gooey. It is not common for a really
good writer to summon up all these negative qualities, though
such instances are not unheard of. In the normal course of
events, however, one would not expect a first-class writer to be
deprived of all these human frailties. He would display some,
hide a few more, and be happily free of the rest. A writer of
farce is in a different position altogether. He can certainly be
amoral, cynical, unprincipled, or ruthlessly detached both
from the gallery of human specimens out of which he draws
his models, and from the emotional gamut of his fictive creatures (this hypothetical case certainly does not apply to Ayckbourn). But he is professionally compelled to be intelligent,
witty, perceptive, alert, sensitive and, above all, quick: in his
pace, mind, action. The shortcomings of the run-of-the-mill
psychological novelist or political playwright are denied to
him. The farceur is safe in the intellectual rigour of his trade.

He runs a different risk however. He can be trivial. This
applies to all and sundry, from Molière to the TV hack. Ayckbourn, like every other writer of farces, does not *always* succeed in avoiding the pitfall of triviality.

Ayckbourn's points of departure are most unprepos-
sessing. Not for him the seedy ferment of an angry terraced
house, but rather the sleepy atmosphere of a semi-detached,
or the sluggish isolation of Annie's decaying mansion in *The
Norman Conquests*. Nothing whatsoever seems to have happened or be likely to happen in these venues of mediocrity
except the abrasive friction of quotidian boredom and the
grinding noise of wear and tear. Out of this unattractive
premise and featureless premises, Ayckbourn spins his cob-
web of interrelated combinations. Whether or not one accepts
him as a serious playwright, there can be little doubt that he
stands peerless as an artificer of plots. *Absurd Person Singular*
witnesses the rise of one married couple and the decline of
another through three successive Christmas Eve Parties in
three different houses, while the third couple undergoes a
gradual reversal of roles between the dominant male and
passive female. *Bedroom Farce* portrays three bedrooms of
couples with fixed abodes and fixed beds, while a fourth

rambling pair, in their candour and innocence, spread havoc and chaos in all the rooms they happen to visit in their peregrinations one restless night. *Just Between Ourselves,* a farce in three acts which all take place in the derelict garage of a detached house, follows the inevitable downfall in a second-hand car's price, a wife's mental equilibrium, and a friend's bank balance caused by the well-meaning interference of a do-it-yourself little man who is determined to repair fuses, car starters, cracked brains and financial failures with the same screwdriver. And then we have the trilogy, now available to an immensely large audience through the slightly vulgarised television programme: a magical combine whereby three distinct and self-sufficient plays interlock round Norman's marital and extra-marital sallies in order to form an epic saga, *The Norman Conquests,* seen from the angle of the dining-room, the lounge and the garden. Once again we have three couples, Norman and Ruth, Reg and Sarah, Tom and Annie, whose unmemorable adventures are triplicated in three different parts of the same house; and the dovetailing of the various components has its own mechanical charm. *Table Manners, Living Together* and *Round and Round the Garden* do not run in a sequence, nor are they simultaneous tales, but they progress concurrently on a precise programme, like a railway time-table, which goes as follows:

Round and Round The Garden	Act I	Scene 1	Saturday	17.30
Table Manners	Act I	Scene 1	Saturday	18.00
Living Together	Act I	Scene 1	Saturday	18.30
Living Together	Act I	Scene 2	Saturday	20.00
Round and Round The Garden	Act I	Scene 2	Saturday	21.00
Table Manners	Act I	Scene 2	Sunday	9.00
Round and Round The Garden	Act II	Scene 1	Sunday	11.00
Table Manners	Act II	Scene 1	Sunday	20.00
Living Together	Act II	Scene 1	Sunday	21.00
Table Manners	Act II	Scene 2	Monday	8.00
Living Together	Act II	Scene 2	Monday	8.00
Round and Round The Garden	Act II	Scene 2	Monday	9.00

The Norman Conquests can be read either as three autonomous two-act four-scene plays, all dealing with the same characters and the same plot, and to be enjoyed on different evenings; or as a whole englobing experience including six acts and twelve scenes to be experienced in chronological sequence. A dogged search in the printed versions for some fracture points between the plots yielded me only two moments when the internal sequence within the single play was slightly at variance with the chronological sequence of the saga. In *Living Together*, Act II, Scene I, the calm conversation between Annie and Sarah follows naturally the previous scene of the same play, but not the scene which precedes it in the chronological order of the trilogy (*Table Manners*, Act II, Scene 1). In that scene, which takes place half an hour before, Tom knocks Norman flat. A similar discrepancy can be noticed in Reg's behaviour in *Round and Round the Garden*, Act II, Scene 2, when he is altogether too bouncy and light-hearted in view of the partial revelation of his wife Sarah's adulterous intentions in the final lines of *Living Together*. Otherwise, each scene runs along on the parallel track of its single and triune entity, contributing at the same time to the resolution of the single play and the completion of the trilogy.

Anyone who has attempted combinatory operations of this kind must know that this is no mean achievement. In the introductory note to the printed text of *Relatively Speaking* (Evans Plays, London, 1968), Ayckbourn modestly places himself in the wake of the Shaftesbury Avenue tradition: "I did set out consciously to write a 'well-made' play. I think this is most important for a playwright to do at least once in his life, since as in any science he cannot begin to shatter theatrical convention or break golden rules until he is reasonably sure in himself what they are and how they were arrived at." Notice the odd word: *science*. The playwright mafia who claim moral superiority and greater professional integrity than the critical mob are kindly requested to pay particular attention. But Ayckbourn is placing himself in the wrong company. The laborious attempts of the "well-made" play school of British dramatists to build up a convincing plot round the trivia of middle-class infatuations have little to do with Ayckbourn's structural acrobatics.

In terms of plot unity, only Shaw can be compared with Ayckbourn's clockwork combines. If instead we pay attention to the latter's search for a plot to defy all plots, an all-encompassing structure which challenges the limitations of narrative and dramatic equilibrium, then only our medieval ancestors knew such ecstasy and underwent such pangs: the visionary embrace of an *Ars Combinatoria* in which all varieties of human emotions and experiences were resolved in a circular unity; or the labours to control an impossibly difficult form, a structure which was beautified by its defiance of any possible mastery, such as the Provençal *sestina*. The content of an Ayckbourn plot sinks towards the vertiginous banality of *Coronation Street,* but its form soars towards the rarefied atmosphere of an aesthete's aesthetics. Joyce, himself a great reader and devotee of medieval poets and philosophers, knew the heady pleasure of a plot which justifies its existence because of its beauty as a plot. In more recent years, only France seems to have nurtured such acolytes of a combinatory mystique. *La disparition* by Georges Pérec, a lipogrammatic novel where what has disappeared is the letter "e" which never occurs in its pages, was dutifully reviewed as a straight novel by a celebrated French critic blissfully unaware of the minor limitation—no use of the letter "e" in the text—that the novelist had set for himself. This bears witness to a fanatic dedication to the cause of narrative experimentation, and Ayckbourn seems to me a writer of the same ilk. The fact that *The Norman Conquests* were also written in order to induce the theatregoer to buy three tickets instead of one and thus treble the playwright's income is equally true.

Apart from these symmetrical schemes with which the playwright, like a modern Houdini, intentionally fetters his freedom of movement in order to prove his command over the theatrical medium, Ayckbourn seems to exploit two main tactical devices: off-stage character and off-stage action—the latter being in his opinion more difficult to handle than the former. Out of view behind the wings, relatives, friends, pet animals, children are allowed to develop larger-than-life features from the safe abode of their absence on the stage. The *minutiae* of daily unimaginative life, which are the exclusive territory of Ayckbourn's on-stage explorations, are thus enlivened and enriched by the more expansive actions of these threatening ghosts who are entitled to be even more ghastly than the characters we come to know in the course of the plays. In *Absent Friends* Paul makes a firm statement about Gordon, Madge's husband, who never appears on the stage: "Nobody's as big as Gordon." Gordon's wife had already compared her husband to a polythene bag full of water. The horror and ugliness of domestic life, so beautifully portrayed in *Absent Friends,* is belittled by this representative of a greater horror and a more distasteful ugliness. The frequent telephonic interventions of this monster of obesity interrupt the sordid action with his own more sordid details (the cough-mixture has spilt on the bed and on the pyjamas; the hot-water bottle is punctured, and so on). "The old sabre-toothed bat," Mother and Mother-in-law, who looms over the proceedings during the weekend of *The Norman Conquests* from her nest upstairs, affects the emotional life of all the guests in the house, although in the trilogy the playwright is not completely successful in conveying the ominous presence of the invisible character through the reactions of the visible ones. By having all the action in the kitchen, *Absurd Person Singular* spares us the sight of another awful couple, loud-mouthed joke-cracking Dick and Lottie, who are lounging in the unseen drawing-rooms during the first two acts; but bestows upon the spectators the vicarious pleasure of hearing that Dick is savagely bitten by another off-stage character, Eva's favourite dog, George, who keeps all her friends unfriendly huddled in the kitchen during the second act by guarding the entrance Cerberus-like. Absent children cast their nasty little shade on the stage in *Mother Figure* (the first sketch of *Confusions,* one of Ayckbourn's most underrated plays) and in *How the Other Half Loves,* where we are continuously fed hair-raising information about Terry's son's devastating activities in the kitchen. Every set is therefore besieged by an aggressive absent figure, be it dog or child or friend or mother-in-law, who contributes to oppress the on-stage characters.

Ayckbourn's most genuine contribution to theatrical technique, however, is his constant recourse to off-stage action. It is like a Velásquez painting which focuses on a peripheral point of reference—the kitchen table with a scullery maid for instance—while the real action is taking place elsewhere in an inconspicuous corner of the canvas. *Absurd Person Singular* shows us a variety of kitchens while parties go on in the lounges. *Bedroom Farce* has three bedrooms, set side by side on the stage, while a festive gathering is roaring underneath one of them. In *Time and Time Again* part of the action occurs on the invisible cricket pitch which witnesses Leonard's defeat and eventual downfall. But the ultimate in off-stage action is of course *The Norman Conquests* in which every single play feeds parasitically on the off-stage action of the other two. As we view the second and then the third play of the trilogy, our awareness of what is going on in the rest of the house and likewise the satisfaction of our curiosity grow concurrently. We enjoy guessing what preceded or what will follow the entrance or the exit of the actor from the garden to the lounge, or from the latter to the kitchen, and we slowly build up a complete picture of the proceedings, as if we were Big Brother enjoying a panoptic and all-embracing vision. I dare surmise that this innovation will count in the future development of theatrical technique.

In farcical plays of this sort it is essential to pitch the action low, down to a base line of utmost banality. The events must ultimately be non-events so as to astonish us with the incomprehensible preoccupations of the characters. The more trifling the occurrences which make the plot move forward, the more hilarious is the shattering effect that these minimal disturbances have upon the emotional lives of our heroes. Trials of strength, tests of character, moral blackmail, psychological pressures, territorial advances or retreats, displays of resistance occur over the adding of milk to a cup of coffee (*Living Together*, I, 2), the purchase of a pair of fancy shoes (*Absent Friends*, Act I), the handing round of sandwiches over tea (both *Absent Friends* and *Just Between Ourselves*).

Look what Ayckbourn manages to extract out of the distribution of seating round the dinner table in *Table Manners*, II, 1 (one of the funniest moments in the trilogy), which becomes both a masterpiece of ceremonial incompetence and the radiography of the power structure of a family group. "I've never pitched anything at such a low key," writes Ayckbourn apropos of *Absent Friends*: but at times all his plays approach a zero degree of action and dialogue. This is at variance with the straight farce tradition in the manner of, say, Feydeau. The typical farce is packed with effervescent dialogue and follows a continuous chain of unexpected events (former or present mistresses appearing or disappearing inside cupboards, jealous husbands pressing at the door either alone or accompanied by their seconds for a duel, visitors turning up unexpectedly from the most unlikely corners of the world to add further confusion, and so on and so forth).

Frantic action is only part of the bag of tricks of Ayckbourn, whose plays also thrive on the absence of any action and on a dialogue verging on inarticulacy. Evelyn in *Absent Friends* describes her own child in terms which come close to the moronic: "'Mmmm"; "Yes"; "He likes it hot"; "He's all right"; "He's not bad," while all the time leafing absentmindedly through women's magazines. Ayckbourn's fumbling idiots (Trevor in *Bedroom Farce*, Tom in *The Norman Conquests*) delight us not only with their hyperbolic blunders but with the poetical rarefaction of their stuttering language, with the exquisite emptiness of their mindless utterances. "Once you get yourself committed to a . . . commitment—like Susannah and I . . . have committed ourselves to, you get a situation of a totally outgoing—non-egotistical—giving—ness . . . a total submerging, you know" (*Bedroom Farce*, Act I). No, we do not know, but we enjoy the fact that he does not succeed in making us know. "It seems to me—we ought to find a way of—well sort out our relationship—if we have one—to such a degree that we—come together more or less on a permanent basis. Temporarily at least . . . Would you like me to marry you? I would. Like me to marry you. May I?" (*Round and Round*, II, 2). The text not only exploits the traditional figure of the slow-witted timid suitor, but the poetry of a language signifying next to nothing even when it purports to represent a major life decision. "Ah well. I'll think of you, wherever you are, mooching about while I'm mooching about here. . . . Funny thing, life!" (*Round and Round*, I, 1). The philosophical remark at the end, "Funny thing, life!," explodes in all its clamorous incongruity because it operates both as an external reference to Tom's stupidity and shyness, and as a self-reference to its own tautological sufficiency (life is a funny thing because there are people who say: Funny thing, life). The whole tradition of a "Theatre of Chatting" from Chekhov onwards influences Ayckbourn as much as the convention of French farces and British pantomimes. Sheila: "There's something so majestic about trees, isn't there?" Greg: "Regal!" (*Relatively Speaking*, I, 2). Madge: "You know me . . . oh, guess what I did get? . . . are you ready? . . . Brace yourself, I got the shoes" (*Absent Friends*, Act I). As Heidegger suggested, people chat in order to demonstrate that they are alive. The characters in Ayckbourn, always on the verge of emptiness in their lives and in their minds, cling persistently to this ephemeral manifestation of existence: chat.

But language is a delicate instrument and often turns treacherous, biting the very tongue that has uttered it. Annie: "Norman, do I look even remotely fragile?" Norman: "I meant mentally fragile" (*Table Manners*, II, 1). Annie: "You can get as drunk as you like. . . ." Norman: "Oh, great! Would you mind if I dropped dead?" (*Table Manners*, II, 1). The whole range of linguistic traps, equivocations, gaffes, unintentional double-entendres, blunders is available to these clumsy manipulators of words. Norman: "What she needs is a bit of the old boot." Tom: "Oh, come on. Boot?" Norman: "Metaphorical." Tom: "Oh, metaphorical boot. What's that exactly?" (*Living Together*, I, 1).

I like that *exactly*, showing the man's terror of words which do not have an *exact* meaning. But language is never exact; on the contrary, it is a constant threat to the pusillanimous characters' diligent attempt to cope with the difficulty of life. At times, language is also an instrument of total falsehood, rising towards peaks of sycophancy. Geoff, the philandering architect, talking about husbands who settle down to a peaceful existence with their wives: "Do you think I don't envy that? . . . God, how I envy them that!" (*Absurd Person Singular*, Act II). Norman: "I'd like to see you happy, Sarah. . . . I'd very much like to make you happy" (*Table Manners*, II, 2). Harry, commenting about the perfume of his *gorgeous* drinking companion: "Very very nice. Very very nice indeed" (*Confusions*, sketch 2). These are occasions when a sequence of trite words has more bite than a well-turned phrase or a brilliant metaphor. Ayckbourn knows how to operate dramatically on what seems to be utterly banal: which is certainly more difficult than the exploitation of the sublime.

My zeal to defend the "seriousness" of Alan Ayckbourn's humour has pushed my interpretation away from the fundamental funniness of his plays. Of course, all his works are good fun in the old farcical tradition, though there has been a considerable change in his treatment of humour from his first plays to *Absent Friends* or *Absurd Person Singular*. In his introduction to *Relatively Speaking* he explains how he came about to write it. Someone has asked him "for a play which would make people laugh when their seaside summer holidays were spoiled by the rain and they came into the theatre to get dry before trudging back to their landladies. This seemed to me as worthwhile a reason for writing the play as any, so I tried to comply." In fact *Relatively Speaking* is very close to the world of undiluted farce, based as it is on a prolonged equivocation which induces Greg to visit his fiancée's former mature lover in the false belief that he is her father. The play exploits all the possible embarrassments that can be caused by such a mistake in the tradition of a comedy of errors which goes back to antiquity.

Even the more recent plays abound with the basic element of theatrical humour, that is incongruity, the association of unassociable elements. Norman: "This lettuce is superb. Whoever cooked it. . . ." (*Table Manners*, II, 1). Long ago Paul had stolen his fiancée's napkin for sentimental reasons; now Evelyn addresses her husband John: "You nicked my uncle's screwdriver!" (*Absent Friends*, Act II). Wife: "My husband has always been old. When he was young he was old" (*Countdown*). The last quotation already points to the cruel world of Ayckbourn's latest farces. In his drawing and dining rooms life is mean and horrible. People are hoping not for a dirty, but a filthy weekend (*Round and Round*, I, 1). They bicker over their soup to see who received too much of it (*Table Manners*, II, 1). Cuckold husbands accept their wives' infidelity in order not to jeopardise their promotion (*Confusions*, sketch 3) or their petty business transactions (*Absent Friends*). Women are described in the same impersonal fashion as properties for sale (*Round And Round*, I, 1). "We are the most miserable family you are ever likely to meet" whines John to Colin in *Absent Friends,* but the record is far from secure because of other contenders in Ayckbourn's world. As for the kitchens of his plays, they are infested by little women with a mania for cleanliness who get their satisfaction out of scrubbing a dirty oven (the first act of *Absurd Person Singular* is in fact a frightening description of the horrors of tidiness). But there's worse to come in the bedrooms, which are a complete disaster. Jan complains about Nick's impotence (*Bedroom Farce,* Act I) and Malcolm gets a stunning answer to an intimate question: "You don't get bored with me?" Kate: "No. No. Not often. . . . Only once or twice." The only remedy seems to be for Malcolm to come to bed in a funny hat (*Bedroom Farce,* Act II). Evelyn, who just "did it" in the back of a car with Diana's husband, comments on his performance: "Horrible. Worse than my husband and that's saying a lot" (*Absent Friends,* Act I). Making love is something to get off our chests, out of our system, like a laxative (*Round And Round*, I, 1). Only Trevor in *Bedroom Farce* and Norman in the trilogy seem to emerge not totally destroyed by the erotic catastrophe. But there is something worse than the pusillanimity of the characters' social life, the fastidiousness of their domestic arrangements, the inadequacy of their sexual experience: and this is the outpouring of pious sentiments from the heart of a well-intentioned yet basically stupid man. Ayckbourn has invented some of the best idiots in the history of modern theatre (Tom, the rambling vet in *The Norman Conquests*; Trevor, the public menace in *Bedroom Farce*), but his greatest creation seems to me Colin in *Absent Friends*: a character who is so well-meaning in his sickly unctuous sentimentality that he carries laughter to the borderline of disgust (two characters in the play get a fit of hysteria just by listening to his cant). And this is obviously far beyond the traditional boundaries of farce.

In fact it would be enough to modify the angle of vision—or perhaps to alter the style of production and acting—in order to obtain plays which would emerge as dolorous examples of human failure, though enlivened by a rich array of humorous remarks. Almost every character in Ayckbourn's plays is a victim of circumstances, or of his own ineptitude, and he or she always deserves a moment of self-revelation with gentle unobtrusive pathos. Here is Norman talking to bitchy Sarah: "Are you happy then?" Sarah: "Yes—mostly. Occasionally. Now and then. I don't know. I don't have time to think about it" (*Living Together*, I, 1). Her kind of down-trodden husband, Reg: "But when I sit here in this house and listen to the quiet. You know, I wonder why I left. I had my own room here, you know. All my books, my own desk, a shelf for my hobbies. . . . I'd make these balsa wood aeroplanes. Dozens of them. Very satisfying. Mind you, they never flew. Soon as I launched them—crack. . . . But it didn't really matter. It was a hell of a bore winding them up" (*Table Manners*, I, 1). Reg's sister, Annie: "[We talk] about super exciting things like does the kitchen ceiling need another coat, and distemper . . . and foot and mouth. Then I pot Mother and retire to bed—alone—itching" (*Table Manners*, I, 1). Marion complaining about her past beauty: "How could anything be so cruel? How could anything be so unutterably cruel?" (*Absurd Person Singular*, Act III). And the examples could be multiplied.

All this is quite at variance with the remarks by a well-known critic who once described Ayckbourn in a *Dictionary of Contemporary Dramatists* as a pure farceur: "His sole aim is to make us laugh. His plays contain no message, offer no profound vision of the universe, tell us nothing about how to live our lives." Leaving aside the profound vision, my opinion happens to be exactly the opposite. In *Mother Figure*, the first sketch of *Confusions*, a woman has lived for so long alone with her children that she even talks to her neighbours as if they were infants. Her conversation is full of choccy bics, smack the botty, toothypegs, lovely choccy and Mr. Poddle. In the adult context I found each word from this baby language terrifying. For reasons which I could not quite fathom the audience was rolling with laughter.

Peter Shaffer's *Equus:* A Review

by Walter Kerr

A true myth is a true bind. All the facts are in, and there is
no way out. Oedipus, an honorable man, can do whatever he
likes to avoid fulfilling the prophecy that he will kill his father
and marry his mother, but he will kill his father and marry his
mother. We give assent to the unresolvable, see that it is
perfectly proportioned, perfectly just, perfectly terrifying.

If there is one thing more than another that a contemporary playwright would like to do, it is to make a myth. We
feel a desperate need these days for new icons, images, clothed
symbols that will help us come to terms with the "dark cave of
the psyche," the cave that thousands of years of reasoning
haven't quite lighted after all.

We want a picture of ourselves that renders us whole,
with all of the violent contraries and inexplicable self-betrayals
locked in. Not an explanation but an intuition become flesh;
not thinking, *seeing.* But, it turns out, myths are extraordi-
narily hard to make, just by the willing of it. We are used to
thinking now, used to explaining before we really see, and it's
not easy to wheel about and go back to magic.

The closest I have seen a contemporary play come—it is
powerfully close—to reanimating the spirit of mystery that
makes the stage a place of breathless discovery rather than a
classroom for rational demonstration is Peter Shaffer's remarkable "Equus," . . . in repertory at the British National

Theater. Mr. Shaffer is the author of "The Royal Hunt of the
Sun," and he may have been trying for just such iconogra-
phy—a portrait of the drives that lead men to crucify
themselves—there. Here, I think, he has found it.

He's done it by using reason to despair of reason. We
begin in what looks like a lecture lab, a handy enough arena
for dissecting the brain: the center space is railed off, some
members of the audience are seated above it on-stage as
though they'd come for a scholarly demonstration. It also
looks, vaguely, like a horse-ring in which winners might be put
through their paces. Then we notice that there are indeed
horses about: from the rungs of steel ladders at both sides of
the stage hang the silvered-frame skeletons of horses' heads.
They are handsome. They are already, as John Napier has
exquisitely designed them, in some way haunting.

A doctor is waiting for a patient, one he doesn't want to
take on. He is weary and wary of tampering with the psyches
of children, though that is his job. The patient is 17, a part-
time stable boy. He has rammed a metal spike through the
eyes of six horses. It is the gratuitous, unfathomable horror of
the act that leads the doctor to accept the charge.

At once we are lured, with infinite skill, into a psychiatric
detective story, the tensions of which account for half the
evening's force. Clues are grudgingly, suspensefully come by.
The defiant boy, blond curls framing a face of stone, won't
speak, he will only mockingly hum television commercials
when prodded. At last tricked into speech by adroit man-
euver, he strikes a sly bargain he means to hold to. For every
question of the doctor's that he answers, the doctor must
answer one of his. Candor for candor, if we're going to get
anywhere.

The process yields tantalizing bits of information. When
he was a child his mother read to him—history, the New
Testament, stories of horses in which horses spoke and felt.
Under his mother's tutelage the boy has become religious
enough to tack a cheap lithograph of the suffering Jesus, feet
chained, back under the lash, to his wall. His atheist father,

enraged, has torn it down and replaced it with the photograph of a horse, head-on, eyes staring.

A suspicion grows that horse and Christ have become one, the chains of the Saviour the bit between the horse's teeth. The boy not only learns to love horses but to adore them: he is caught once by his father with wire forced into his own mouth, slashing at his body with a riding-crop. On dark nights he slips into the stable, strips himself, and goes riding in the fields, sexually excited, joined to his god, self-made centaur.

But all the while that we are fitting bits and pieces together, still far from the sight of any answer, the questioning process has turned up something else: the hopelessly chained soul of the doctor himself. Alec McCowen plays the role: I doubt that he has ever done anything half so brilliant. Tie loose, eyes tired, he is suddenly vulnerable. One of the questions fired at him by the boy, which ought to be answered if the bargain is to be kept, is capable of infuriating him. Does he have any sex with his wife? In an unprofessional temper, he dismisses the boy for the day.

Yet the rage is other than it seems. In point of fact Mr. McCowen has no sex at all, having married an antiseptic Scotch lady dentist: they "briskly wooed, briskly wed, were briskly disappointed, and turned briskly to their respective surgeries." It is his own surgery—his genuine capacity for returning young minds to accepted norms—that frightens him. He dreams, on his unluckier nights, that he is Agamemnon applying the sacrificial scalpel to long lines of children, all waiting to have imagination, passion, individuality taken out of them. He is jealous of the boy he means to cure, jealous of his madness. While he, with his pallid fondness for all things Greek, has leafed drawings of centaurs, the boy has become one. There is a bit between his own teeth that will never come out.

Civilization and its discontents again. Yes. And, as we move into the equally arresting second half of the play, on our way to the metal spike, we are not only aware that the theme is a common enough one in our time, we are also inclined—out of our restless logical impulses—to challenge, or at least think twice about, certain of the icon's ambiguities. Wishing for sex with a girl, the boy is temporarily impotent: "The Lord thy God is a jealous God." Only if the all-seeing god is blinded can the boy take a second step. Questions bother us here: Is it wrong to cure impotence, wrong to kill a false and hurtful equation between one pair of eyes and another? And hasn't the decision to reject his god, to be no longer a centaur, been the boy's rather than the doctor's?

But that is logic at work again—really work for the next day, not while the second act is actually exerting its spell—and it is to be at least temporarily dismissed in view of the fact that the structure, the two terrible tensions pulling in contrary directions, the sense of myth slowly disclosing itself, all do really function in the theater. They function in part because Mr. Shaffer has done his own work with the precision of Agamemnon's scalpel, in part because Mr. McCowen commands us to believe without reserve in the agony and honesty of his man (Peter Firth, as the boy, keeps pace perfectly with his mentor), and in part because director John Dexter has been able to make the experience intensely visual.

There is, for instance, a superb effect at the first act climax, the night-ride of a boy and horse unleashed. We might only have heard of this; it could have been narrated. A film would do it literally and, I think, lose intensity in the doing. Here the boy simply mounts the shoulders of one of the six shadowy figures who have from time to time during the evening slipped beneath the brooding horses' masks. The hooves of the boy's alter ego begin to paw the stage floor: they are spiky silver elevations that look like inverted jeweled crowns.

Then the stage floor itself begins to move, turned on its axis by the nodding, neighing horse-men at hand so that the railings at first slip by, then race by. With the exultation of the boy's passion, the increasing speed of the spinning ground, the rush of air that both seem to generate as track whirls away beneath the silver, we are left not only persuaded but spellbound by the clattering, crying, crop-whipping authenticity of the image.

Over-all, it is the image that stands, and is complete. The

boy, with his dangerous creativity, fills one half of it, forever driven, forever blocked. The doctor fills the other, feverishly unwilling to do what he must do, doing it—only to block himself. The two fit together at unpredictable angles, like differently colored pieces in a stained-glass window, but they fit and use up all the space that there is. Any move either makes destroys the other. Locked horns, both right, no escape. The play is perfectly proportioned to its mutual pain.

We have been looking for craftsmanship like this for a long time.

The Political Spectrum
of Edward Bond:
from Rationalism to Rhapsody

by Christopher Innes

The landmarks in contemporary English drama have been more like landmines, shattering conventional expectations, with a whole new configuration of subjects and themes emerging on the stage each time after the dust of public outrage settled. What *Look Back in Anger* had done for the fifties, *Saved* did for the sixties, and a play like *The Romans in Britain* may yet do for the eighties (though Howard Brenton's play seems to lack the qualities that might give its shock effects the same resonance). Like Osborne, Edward Bond achieved immediate prominence through the controversy surrounding his first play to be given a full production, when the Lord Chamberlain tried to throw a baby out with the bath-water. But where Osborne quickly became accepted—partly because his approach was relatively simple and consistent, partly because his plays were recognizably traditional in shape, despite his use of diatribe which shifted dramatic conflict from its conventional locus between characters within the play to a point between his protagonists and the audience—there is still little consensus about Bond.

Initially Bond was subjected to perhaps the most violent storm of protest and denigration aimed at any modern dramatist since Ibsen. Indeed, the reaction to *Saved* paralleled the original English response to *Ghosts,* even down to the vocabulary. Ibsen's "abominable play" had been condemned half a century earlier as "gross, almost putrid indecorum . . . literary carrion" (*Daily Telegraph*), with "characters either contradictory in themselves, uninteresting or abhorrent" (*Daily Chronicle*); in short, "a piece to bring the stage into disrepute and dishonour with every right-thinking man and woman" (*Lloyds*). Bond's play was attacked as being "not . . . the feeblest thing I have seen on any stage, but . . . certainly the nastiest . . ." (J. C. Trewin, *Illustrated London News,* 13 Nov. 1965), with "characters who, almost without exception are foul-mouthed, dirty-minded, illiterate and barely to be judged on any recognizable human level at all" (H. Kretzmer, *Daily Express,* 4 Nov. 1965). Meanwhile, members of the general public formed pressure groups to mobilize opinion against such pornographic, sadistic, filthy, "unfunny and obscene" plays as *Saved.*[1] At first glance this seems an unjustified over-reaction. Babies are slaughtered on stage in revered classical tragedies. Degraded dregs of society had been an accepted focus for serious plays from Gorki's *The Lower Depths* or Büchner's *Woyzeck* to Gelber's *The Connection.* The "kitchen sink" was almost a commonplace in English drama after Osborne.

Still, in contrast to the general reaction, leading theatre people and critics like Olivier, Tynan, Bryden, Esslin and Mary McCarthy recognized that *Saved* was not only strikingly original, but a deeply moral work. And with his truly impressive output of ten full-length plays, four adaptations, an opera and various short pieces in the last fifteen years, Bond is now widely accepted as the single most important contemporary British dramatist. Yet, apart perhaps from *The Sea* and *Bingo,* critical acclaim has hardly been matched by popular appreciation. In fact, the most striking thing about the stage history of even his most major work is its relative neglect by the English-speaking theatre. Up to 1977 there were only eighteen productions of *Saved* and a bare six productions of *Lear* throughout Britain, the United States, Canada, New Zealand and

[1]Mary V. Thom, Letter on *Saved, Plays and Players,* 13, No. 5 (Feb. 1966), 6.

Australia, as compared to fifty-eight and seventeen in other countries[2]—statistics which can be put into perspective by a further comparison. Within three years of its opening, a play like Peter Shaffer's *Equus* achieved over double the number of productions, and whereas the longest English run of *Lear* was just over one month, *Equus* was given 131 performances at the Old Vic and ran for over two years on Broadway.

Such disparity between Bond's reputation and his public exposure has created what could be called a critical credibility gap. Certainly it raises questions with which few studies of Bond have yet attempted to deal. To some extent, it might be put down to apparent obscurity, since even among those critics who established his reputation there has been little consensus about how his themes should be interpreted. To some extent, too, it is a measure of the deliberately unsettling effect of Bond's plays. But far more, it seems due to the contradictory and changing nature of his approach: his demand for objective analysis while simultaneously provoking emotion, and in particular his shift from what he labelled as "rational theatre" to "rhapsody." If we trace Bond's development from his first series of plays, ending with *The Sea*, through his second series, which runs from *Bingo* to *The Woman*, it becomes clear that this shift has radically changed the terms of his social criticism. As a result, the criteria established by early plays are totally inappropriate to his later work. However, this modulation seems to have gone generally unrecognized, because Bond himself either refuses to acknowledge the reversal of his earlier principles, or takes steps to disguise the change.

The coherence of Bond's prefaces, which repeat and elaborate a highly specific social analysis, gives his work a misleading impression of consistency. He also takes care to underline the impression by gathering all of his major plays into a double series, in each of which bleak presentations of contemporary problems and their historical roots end in a positive statement of hope, with one play from the first series being rewritten to fit into the second as *The Bundle . . . or New*

[2]Malcolm Hay and Philip Roberts, *Edward Bond: A Companion to the Plays* (London, 1978), pp. 79–85, 90–3.

Narrow Road to the Deep North, and with the imposition of formal uniformity on the second series through the use of parallel subtitles: "Scenes of Money and Death," "Scenes of Bread and Love," "Scenes of Right and Evil," "Scenes of Freedom." The apparent consistency is marked, too, by the way the same images surface in different plays—in particular, Bond's central thematic symbol, the symbiotic pairing of protagonists, which reappears from Scopey and the hermit whom he replaces by murdering in *The Pope's Wedding,* through the Siamese twins of *Early Morning,* to Hecuba and Ismene in *The Woman.* In a simple reversal of Ibsen's *Ghosts,* where society's dead haunt the living, Bond's society of "ghosts in chains" is haunted by the "pro-life" half of each pair, representing conscience. Since no one can totally escape the deadly effect of social conditioning, in Bond's earlier plays the positive qualities of these figures are indeed ghostly: "The pro-life half of the pairs . . . has been killed off like the others . . . but not completely killed." In his later plays they become dominant. Yet the scale, by which moral survival can be measured, remains constant throughout. At one extreme is active resistance to society: for instance, the assassination of Heros, the authority figure in *The Woman.* At the mid-point on the scale are symbolic acts of resistance which function as moral examples and lead to imitation: Lear's final gesture of digging up the wall he built as king, or Arthur's refusal to participate in the cannibal competitiveness of *Early Morning.* At the other extreme is Len's minimum of "restless curiosity" in *Saved,* which in one sense has to be seen as highly ambiguous—a morbid and voyeuristic fascination with murder—yet for Bond "amounts to the search for truth, and in the contexts in which . . . [Scopey and Len] find themselves it's miraculous!"[3]

On this level, Bond's social analysis has the coherence of simplicity. Social institutions, originally developed for the protection of individuals, become self-perpetuating. Law and religion, mores and morality, now have no other function but moulding individuals to serve their needs. Such repression

[3]Edward Bond, "Letters to Irene," 7 January 1970, in Hay and Roberts, p. 43.

leads to aggression, and this aggression is the driving force behind social progress. Thus, all social activity is presented as moralized violence. The sack of Troy that the authorities condone, or the anarchic murder and rape of civil war in *Lear,* the politically justified killing of the children in *Narrow Road,* or the socially condemned stoning of a baby in *Saved*—all are treated as actions of exactly the same kind and status. For Bond, violence is not an aberration but a general symptom. The infanticide for which Fred is sent to prison is no different from his beating by ordinary housewives who represent the moral outrage in the judicial system which condemns him. Indeed, the way Bond manipulates such parallels makes the point overly obvious:

> *Fred.* Bloody 'eathens. Thumpin' and kickin' the van.
>
> ....
> I don't know what'll 'appen. There's bloody gangs like that roamin' everywhere. The bloody police don't do their job.[4]

Fred's criminal act is presented as a logical extension of social norms, a point also indicated by the parodistic references to disciplining children and toilet-training in the baby-killing sequence itself. But this symptom is also intended to act as a symbol ("the Massacre of the Innocents") on quite a different level, and Bond's parade of children who are stoned, put to the sword, or thrown from the battlements of an emblematic Troy is designed to image what social conditioning does to us all. For Bond,

> All our culture, education, industrial and legal organization is directed to the task of killing [people psychologically and emotionally]. .... Education is nothing less than corruption, because it's based on institutionalizing the pupil, making him a decent citizen.[5]

Following this analysis, we are all victims; and the rulers are as repressed as those they exploit. Indeed, aggressors need to be even more strictly conditioned to function socially than those they oppress. So where Bond creates symbolic authority fig-

---

[4]Edward Bond, *Saved,* in *Plays: One* (London, 1977), pp. 83 and 85.
[5]Bond, "Letter to Irene," pp. 43–4.

ures, like the monstrous imperialist Georgina, they are presented as insane.

Perhaps the clearest dramatic statement of these themes is not *Narrow Road to the Deep North,* which deals with the mechanics of oppression, but *Early Morning,* which explains its mentality. It is perhaps understandable, Bond's aim being to document the delusions of a sick society, that a critic like Esslin should have interpreted *Early Morning* as a fantasy, treating its cannibalism as an "expression of the earliest infantile sexuality," oral eroticism," the Siamese twins as "an image of childhood too: sibling rivalry . . . ," and the play itself as "a dream world of infant sexuality."[6] In reaction to this kind of approach, Bond insists that *Early Morning* is "social realism." This seems a fairly arbitrary use of critical labels, but underlines that the play is intended to be a realistic demonstration of the psychology that perpetuates and justifies political power structures, an objective record of subjective illusions:

> What we perceive really isn't a straight transcription of reality, and because people do live in fantasy worlds that is part of social reality. If we could understand our problems, we wouldn't have any need of mythologies and absurd religions to close that gap. . . .
> . . . .
> I am writing about the pressures of the past that are misforming our present time, and that's where it received its public image and its normative values. . . .[7]

Thus, Victorian morality is seen as the legitimation of contemporary political and economic institutions, while Queen Victoria's lesbianism stands for the perversion of an individual's personality by power. The Siamese twins are the social versus the moral (and anarchist) halves of a single character. "Heaven" is the popular concept translated straight into socio-economic terms: a state in which those desires desig-

---

[6]Martin Esslin, "A Bond Honoured," *Plays and Players,* 15, No. 9 (June 1968), 26.

[7]Edward Bond and Christopher Innes, "Edward Bond: From Reationalism to Rhapsody," *Canadian Theatre Review,* No. 23 (Summer 1979), 109 and 111.

nated as "good" by the inverted morality of society can be indulged without consequence.

What the play demonstrates as well, however, is an unintentional confusion of categories that also characterizes the arguments in some of Bond's prefaces. On one level, the structure of the play is a straight-line story from Albert's palace revolution, through civil war and the deaths of all the characters, to afterlife and Arthur's "ascension." On another level, the structure corresponds to the maturing moral vision of the protagonist: Act I, childhood, where Arthur can make no sense of the self-destructive repressiveness of the establishment or its equally appalling alternatives; Act II, adolescence, where Arthur, now conditioned to accept social practices, carries them through to their logical end (the final solution, as it were, which also stands for the holocaust of nuclear war that Bond sees as the inevitable consequence if aggressive societies continue along their present lines); and Act III, adulthood, where Arthur recognizes the true nature of society and rejects it. At the same time, on a third level, the final Act is a symbolic restatement of the earlier actions—having been shown particular examples of society in action, we are then given a universalized analysis of their inner meaning. Quite apart from the overlap of conflicting perspectives, there is a serious inconsistency here. The reciprocal cannibalism of "heaven" is both an image of capitalist free enterprise and a symbol of the way "people consume each other emotionally . . . in a society where there's only taking";[8] and the first two Acts have demonstrated that there is no escape from or exception to this. Yet on the symbolic level, the very character who is totally socially conditioned and who takes the death principle of society to its logical conclusion, is able to refuse to eat. Not only that: by apparent osmosis or some undefined form of sympathetic magic, his passive example not only spreads temporary indigestion (or pangs of conscience) through the whole

⁸Edward Bond and Walter Asmus, "Die Gesellschaft erzieht die Menschen zu Mördern: Interview mit Edward Bond,' *Theater Heute*, 10, No. 11 (Nov. 1969).

society, but also (rather more logically) starts a chain reaction of conversion with Florence, who is brought to question society's assumptions—"Perhaps I'm alive, perhaps we needn't be like this"—and ends by finding excuses for not eating other people.[9] This conversion is intended, of course, as a model for the future behaviour of Bond's audience. Yet all the preceding events have demonstrated nothing but the inevitability of the corruption, perversion or destruction of any instinctive moral goodness by social conditioning—so much so, that the very existence of a positive character in the context Bond has created means that the playwright must have overstated his case against society. As a result, either his social analysis is questionable, or his solution must be seen as wish-fulfillment.

It might be possible to dismiss this contradiction as simply the effect of an over-ambitious play, where the playwright has been unable to synthesize his material or provide a coherent perspective. But Bond himself sets *Early Morning* both technically and thematically above plays like either *Saved* or *Narrow Road*. In addition, exactly the same problem recurs in other plays: for example, the naked man who rescues himself at the end of *Narrow Road,* or the depiction of Len in *Saved,* which Bond has recognized as "almost irresponsibly optimistic."[10] Indeed, his attempts to resolve this paradox in his later plays makes his social criticism seem more rather than less contentious; and Bond is so clearly a didactic dramatist that the validity of his message largely determines the quality of his theatre.

This statement is particularly true, since he has defined his aim in general terms as taking the audience "through the learning process of the characters' lives." In *Early Morning*, this aim conditions even the style of presentation. On yet another level, the play is written from Arthur's viewpoint: Act I is deliberately bewildering because "he is bewildered by the political set-up and his own emotional involvement in it . . ."; Act II, grotesque because he is mad; and Act III, "simple and

[9]Edward Bond, *Early Morning,* in *Plays: One,* pp. 211 and 223.

[10]Edward Bond, Harold Hobson et al., "A Discussion with Edward Bond," *Gambit,* 5, No. 17 (1970), 32; and Bond, *Plays: One,* p. 309.

direct . . . because . . . Arthur recovers his sanity. . . ."[11] This learning process is nowhere so literal in Bond's other plays. But whatever the merits or limitations of indoctrination through imitation, Bond's analysis of society itself calls his didactic aims into question on a much more fundamental level.

If we are all socially conditioned victims, exploiters and exploited alike, and therefore functionally insane, whom can he address? Bond implies that only those, like himself, who have managed to escape the educational process, are capable of perceiving reality. According to him, the fact that he was prevented from taking the grammar school entrance examination "was the making of me. . . . [A]fter that nobody takes you seriously. The conditioning process stops. Once you let them send you to grammar school and university, you're ruined."[12] This view leads him to highly contentious conclusions, such as the statement that "It is impossible for the upper class to create poetry now. You can only have working-class poetry; the rest is rubbish."[13] Yet, almost by definition, theatre audiences nowadays are educated. There were earlier examples of the search for a working-class audience, ranging from Joan Littlewood's establishment of a theatre in Stratford East to Arnold Wesker's Trades Union links in Centre 42, if Bond had wished to follow them. But apart from occasional pieces written for CND rallies or the Anti-Apartheid Movement, Bond's plays demand the resources and acting skills of the professional theatre with its predominantly middle-class public. And this demand is implicitly recognized within the plays. After *Saved,* very few of Bond's positive figures are proletarian. Even in *The Woman,* where an escaped slave kills the power figure responsible for setting up an unjust social structure, it is Queen Hecuba who initiates and controls this revolutionary action.

[11]Edward Bond, "Letter to Ruth Leeson," 14 January 1977, and "About 'Early Morning': Letter to Michael Whitaker," 6 November 1969, in Hay and Roberts, pp. 67 and 50.

[12]Bond, quoted in Hay and Roberts, p. 7.

[13]Bond and Innes, 113.

The usual problem with didactic drama is that it preaches to the converted. Bond, by contrast, seems to be addressing the inconvertible (in his terms); and this may explain certain elements in his plays that are otherwise confusing. For example, Bond labels his work "rational theatre,"[14] yet madness is one of his major themes, and his images are almost unprecedented in their visceral effect. Moreover, in *The Woman* rationalism itself seems to be dismissed, and Pericles' Athens is presented solely as a slave state.

Perhaps the best way of clarifying this paradox is to compare Bond's approach with that of Brecht, who also referred to his theatre as a "rational" one. On the surface the links are clear: Bond began at the Royal Court with exercises in Brechtian dramaturgy; he worked on updating *Roundheads and Peaked Heads*; he arranged an evening of Brecht songs (which have similarities in tone and form to his own poetry); and he admits that *Narrow Road* and *Saved* are "somewhat Brechtian in shape. . . ." But the impression that Bond is a direct follower of Brecht seems mainly due to the fact that William Gaskill directed the first productions of almost all Bond's plays up to *Bingo;* and Gaskill has described his own directorial style as being "as clinically accurate as possible . . . a legacy from the influence of Brecht. . . ."[15] Some critics indeed noted the incongruity of "Brechtian sparseness" to *Early Morning*. But their demand for "more visual fantasy"[16] proved in the event to be equally misleading. For instance, when Peter Stein produced *Early Morning* in Zürich, the setting was indeed grotesque and fantastical, with distorted perspectives and surrealistic effects. Victoria sat on an elaborate throne, like a tennis umpire's chair perched on a ladder, in a room of melting architectural shapes, with seemingly organic and sinisterly womblike walls. In the garden-party scene, the actors were dwarfed by a gigantic folding deck-chair extending up into the flies, which became successively a gallows, a moun-

[14]See Bond and Innes, 112.
[15]Bond and Hobson, 35; and William Gaskill and Irving Wardle, "Interview with William Gaskill," *Gambit,* 5, No. 17 (1970), 41.
[16]Ronald Bryden, *Observer,* 16 March 1969, p. 26. Cf. also Esslin, "First Nights: *Early Morning,*" *Plays and Players,* 16, No. 8 (May 1969), 26.

tain, a mausoleum. The effect of this hallucinatory illusion was to shift the play's viewpoint to inside the mad world, so that Arthur's insanity became its norm, with the result that Zürich critics were led to think that "Bond wants total negation," because "the only humanly possible society is one that is definitively dead. Only when there are no more men does man have a chance."[17]

Bond himself insists that "Very little scenery should be used, and in the last six scenes probably none at all," limiting even a throne-room to *"a bench, upstage, and downstage two chairs or a smaller bench. ...."*[18] But this is the bareness of abstraction rather than Brechtian demonstration; simplification and imaginative suggestion rather than Brecht's open theatricality with the stage machinery exposed and actors stepping out of role.

In fact, what Bond shares with Brecht is not so much a theatrical form as the attitude which he has described in Brecht's work as a certain optimistic "naïvety" that "covers painful knowledge"[19] (what Brechtian critics have labelled "romanticism") and the same philosophical starting-point. For Brecht, personality is not innate, but determined by social function. The exploitive class system of capitalism imposes the strain of being evil on men, making the natural instinct to goodness a fearful temptation to be avoided because self-destructive. Bond has restated Brecht's viewpoint almost exactly:

> For me people are naturally good or rather, it is natural for them to be good *or* bad. What they are depends upon their society. I believe that in a good society it is "natural" for them to be kind. If they are evil, that too has to be created.[20]

[17]Werner Wollenberger, *Zürcher Weltwoche*, 10 October 1969; [all translations in this chapter are by Christopher Innes—Ed.]

[18]Bond, *Early Morning*, pp. 138 and 146.

[19]Edward Bond, "Drama and the Dialectics of Violence," *Theatre Quarterly*, 2 No. 5 (1972), 13, quoted in Peter Holland, "Brecht, Bond, Gaskill, and the Practice of Political Theatre," *Theatre Quarterly*, 8, No. 30 (Summer 1978), 27.

[20]Bond, quoted in Hay and Roberts, p. 26.

Brecht's epic techniques, however, were a response to the circumstances of a specific time and place—Germany and the rise of fascism. His ideals of objectivity, distancing and rationality were explicitly intended as what Brecht later called "a withdrawal course for emotional drug addicts":[21] an antidote to the rhetorical emotionalism and sentimentalized heroic posturing of the Nazis, who claimed Wagner as the sacred expression of the national soul. For Bond, writing for a different era and a generation who appeared to accept violence with complacent calmness, the needs of the sixties and seventies were very different. So, while acknowledging Brecht's influence, Bond sees his theatrical approach as "outdated."[22]

In this, interestingly, Bond parallels such contemporary German dramatists as Franz Xaver Kroetz or Heiner Müller. To Kroetz, the major contemporary problem is the "speechlessness" of the socially exploited who have been deprived of the verbal ability to manipulate or even recognize their situation, whereas "Brecht's figures are so fluent," having "a fund of language . . . which is not in fact conceded to them by their rulers," that "the way is open to a positive utopia, to revolution."[23] So, in contrast to Brecht's, Kroetz's characters use a truncated and brutalized dialogue very reminiscent of the speech in *Saved*. Similarly, Müller rejected Brecht's rational objectivity for violent images that would arouse immediate, emotional reactions because "the time for intervening to alter something is always less. Consequently there is really no more time for discursive dramaturgy, for a calm presentation of factual content."[24] Commenting on his version of *Lear,* Bond referred to precisely the same sense of urgency: "Shakespeare had time. He must have thought that in time certain changes

[21]Bertolt Brecht, quoted in Manfred Wekwerth, "Berliner Ensemble 1968," *Theater Heute*, 9, No. 2 (Feb. 1968), 17.

[22]John Lane, "Resounding Success," *The Times* (London), 25 September 1969, p. 8.

[23]Franz Xaver Kroetz, *Süddeutscher Zeitung*, 20/21 November 1971, p. 4.

[24]Heiner Müller and Horst Laube, "Drama: Die Dramatiker und die Geschichte seiner Zeit; Ein Gespräch," *Theater 1975 (Theater Heute* Sonderheft), p. 120.

would be made. But time has speeded up enormously, and for us, time is running out. . . ."[25] Not surprisingly, then, in contrast to Brecht, Bond uses short, even fragmented scenes to gain intensity, and starkly powerful images for emotional immediacy.

However, the performance values of Bond's theatre are still "rational" in the sense that his experience of staging his own plays convinced him that his scripts require a conceptual approach on the actors' part. In producing *The Woman,* for example, Bond found himself "astonished at the way the acting forced the play into the ground, buried it in irrelevant subjectivity," because the characters were being portrayed in naturalistic emotional terms. So he imposed "a new sort of acting. Put roughly and briefly, it's this. A concept, an interpretation (of the situation, not the character) must be applied to an emotion, and it is this concept or interpretation or idea that is acted. This relates the character to the social event so that he becomes its story teller.[26] This abstracting, intellectualizing quality, of course, in no way reverses Bond's earlier rejection of "anybody who imagines the answers to life are cerebral and that the problems are cerebral." It refers only to the technique of presentation. For the audience, "Theatre involves the whole person. . . . Ideas are two-dimensional . . . involvement on the stage is a three-dimensional process."[27] So the active factor in Bond's theatre is specifically the emotional third dimension—instinctive gut responses.

Even when he defines his work as the objective analysis of society, and therefore "rational," Bond's objectivity does not turn out to have its generally accepted meaning. For Bond, the primary quality that defines art *per se* is "rational objectivity, the expression of the need for interpretation, meaning, order—that is: for a justice that isn't fulfilled in the existing social order."[28] However much we may agree with Bond about

---

[25]Bond, quoted in Hay and Roberts, p. 18.

[26]Edward Bond, "Green Room: Us, Our Drama and the National Theatre," *Plays and Players,* 26, No. 1 (Oct. 1978), 8–9.

[27]Bond and Hobson, 19, and Bond and Innes, 112.

[28]Edward Bond, "The Rational Theatre," in *Plays: Two* (London, 1978), p. xiii.

the irrationality of society, his polemic creation of synonyms should give us pause. Analysed logically, his statement is a syllogism of the simplistic cats have four legs / dogs have four legs / all cats are dogs pattern. It could be laid out as follows: art is objective / attacks on society are objective / all attacks on society are art. (And conversely, no work that accepts any existing social order can qualify as art.) In other words, objectivity is not impartiality but a particular political bias, and a "rational" theatre is a theatre of political persuasion.[29] And remembering that he sees his audience as composed of spiritually dead people, we realize that Bond's function as a playwright has to be the same as Arthur's in the heaven of *Early Morning*: to cause extreme moral discomfort.

This is the effect arrived at in the way Bond uses farce, although some critics tend to treat his comedy in a traditional light as "an intellectual medium, demanding detachment. . . ."[30] But even if this conventional view has some validity for elements of *The Sea* or perhaps *Narrow Road*, the treatment of, say, the Warrington torture scene in *Lear* is much more characteristic.

> *Fontanelle.* Use the boot! *(Soldier A kicks him.)* Jump on him! *(She pushes Soldier A.)* Jump on his head!
> *Soldier A.* Lay off, lady, lay off! 'Oo's killin' 'im, me or you?
> *Bodice (knits).* One plain, two purl, one plain.
> *Fontanelle.* Throw him up and drop him. I want to hear him drop. . . .
> *Bodice (to Soldier A).* Down on your knees.
> *Soldier A.* Me?
> *Bodice.* Down! *(Soldier A kneels.)* Beg for his life.
> *Soldier A (confused).* 'Is? *(Aside.)* What a pair!—O spare 'im, mum.
> *Bodice (knits).* No.

[29]This, of course, is the same definition used by Peter Weiss in *Dramen 2* (Frankfurt, 1968), pp. 468–9, and by Mao Tse-tung in "Talks at the Yenan Forum of Art and Literature" (1942), where he explained that "showing both sides of the question" meant that "every dark force which endangers the masses must be exposed, while every revolutionary struggle of the masses must be praised," and art is "good . . . if it opposes retrogression and promotes progress" (*Drama in the Modern World*, D. A. Heath [1974], pp. 560 and 558).

[30]Richard Scharine, *The Plays of Edward Bond* (Lewisburg, 1976), p. 253.

Soldier A. If yer could see yer way to. 'E's a poor ol' gent, lonely ol'
   bugger. . . .
Bodice. It's my duty to inform you—
Soldier A. Keep still! Keep yer eyes on madam when she talks
   t'yer.
Bodice. —that your pardon has been refused. . . . *(She pokes the
   needles into Warrington's ears.)* I'll just jog these in and out a little.
   Doodee, doodee, doodee, doo.[31]

The incongruity of juxtaposing heartless farce and human
suffering is explicitly intended to be highly disturbing. As
Bond has said, "the effect" of such an "inappropriate" tone "is
very cruel."[32] Indeed, Bond's use of farcical comedy has to be
seen as an extension of his naked images of violence. For
example, on a thematic level, the baby-killing in *Saved* may be
a symbol for social pressures; but in terms of dramatic function, its value is primarily that it provokes extreme reactions in
an audience. As Bond commented: "everybody's reaction is
different . . . people came out absolutely shaking and other
people can't even watch it. So it's their reaction. I mean they
must ask themselves, not ask me what I think about it."[33]

   In fact, the change from graphic realism in *Saved* to the
grand guignol of *Early Morning* or *Lear* is only a response to
the public's capacity for accommodating themselves to violence. As Bond openly admits: "If I went on stoning babies in
every play then nobody would notice it anymore. I had to find
[continually new] ways of making people notice, of making
those things effective. . . ." This is what he has labelled "the
aggro-effect" in deliberate distinction from the Brechtian
"alienation effect":

   In contrast to Brecht, I think it's necessary to disturb an audience emotionally, to involve them emotionally in my plays, so
   I've had to find ways of making that "aggro-effect" more
   complete, which is in a sense to surprise them, to say "Here's a
   baby in a pram—you don't expect these people to stone that
   baby." Yet—snap—they do.[34]

[31]Edward Bond, *Lear,* in *Plays: Two,* pp. 28–9.
[32]Edward Bond, "Letter to Angela Praesent," 25 January 1977, in Hay
and Roberts, p. 72.
[33]Bond, quoted in Hay and Roberts, p. 10.
[34]Bond and Innes, 112 and 113.

By most standards, the power of the emotional reaction to either mode of presentation was all that Bond could have wished. In one of the *Lear* previews, "When the Ghost says 'People will be kind to you now, surely, you've suffered enough,' a departing gentleman in the stalls was heard to remark: "Yes, so have we!' " With *Saved*, one critic "spent a lot of the first act shaking with claustrophobia and thinking I was going to be sick." Indeed, soon this sort of response apparently became exactly what directors of *Saved* aimed at, and the American première was described as a "complete success" almost solely on the grounds that "the walkout rate after the first half was the highest the theatre has ever had, and I have never seen an audience at a traditional play so disturbed. . . ."[35] But for any protagonist, simply provoking a rejection of his message would be obviously counterproductive. So Bond tends also to claim that his farce is designed to control the violence "by irony, so that it would become a focus to jolt the audience into thinking . . . ," and he points out that, because the peak of violence is only half-way through the play, the climax is not the murder itself but the exploration of its causes and effects. These explanations seem to underestimate the power of his images of violence, which tend to produce a form of emotional overkill that makes consequential thought almost impossible. But clearly Bond sees outraging the audience emotionally as a sort of shock therapy designed to galvanize their consciences into life and provoke them into viewing society "objectively" and "rationally" (that is, from his perspective). For him, the degree of violence is nothing more than a measure of urgency, and he denies any "desire to shock."

> The shock is justified by the desperation of the situation or as a way of forcing the audience to search for reasons in the rest of the play. *If* you have the effrontery to say, "I am going to use an aggressive 'aggro-effect' against an audience," if you have the impertinence to say that—and I've just said it—then it must be

[35]Gregory Dark, "Production Casebook No. 5: Edward Bond's 'Lear' at the Royal Court," *Theatre Quarterly*, 2, No. 5 (Jan.–March 1972), 31; Penelope Gilliatt, in *Contemporary Theatre*, ed. Geoffrey Morgan (London, 1968), p. 41; Michael Feingold, "New York 2: Ensembles," *Plays and Players*, 16, No. 8 (May 1969), 65.

because you feel you have something desperately important to tell them. If they were sitting in a house on fire, you would go up to them and shake them violently. . . . And so it's only because I feel it is important to involve people in the realities of life that I sometimes use those effects.[36]

Bond's reuse of the image of "a house on fire" from an interview in 1971 (shortly after *Lear*) in an interview in 1979 (when he was working upon *The Woman*) indicates that his approach to the audience has remained fairly consistent. But beneath this there has been a radical shift in Bond's ideas, starting with his attempt to define the right relationship between writing and politics in *Bingo*; and this shift has changed the nature of his dramaturgy.

One of Bond's major themes—perhaps THE major theme after the "Violence [that] shapes and obsesses our society, . . ." which he claims to "write . . . about as naturally as Jane Austen wrote about manners"[37]—is the role and responsibility of the writer. As early as *Narrow Road*, Bond takes a writer as his protagonist, although here the traditional poet-philosopher figure is simply a contrast to his own position. Basho is an idealist who uses the abstract ideals of art as an excuse for non-involvement, then for atrocities. He provides an image of false culture, a way of attacking the academic or aesthetic approach to literature; and the fact that Basho has been singled out as the only "villain" in Bond's full-length plays perhaps indicates the strength of his conviction about the necessity for an artist to be politically committed. There is even the suggestion that if there were no injustice or oppression, then there would be no reason for art at all: "In an ideal society . . . [Basho] would have picked that baby up, gone off the stage and there would have been no necessity for a play."[38]

This concept of false culture is also implicit in *Lear*, since it was the way Shakespeare had become the epitome and justification of purely aesthetic art that provoked Bond into adapting *King Lear*.

[36]Bond and Innes, 113.
[37]Bond, *Lear*, p. 3.
[38]Bond and Hobson, 9.

... I very much object to the worshipping of that play by the academic theatre ... because I think it is a totally dishonest experience. ... it's an invitation to be artistically lazy to say "Oh, how marvellous sensitive we are and this marvellous artistic experience we're having, understanding this play" ... [so you] don't have to question yourself, or change your society.[39]

It should hardly be surprising, then, to find Bond starting his second sequence of plays with Shakespeare himself as a protagonist. Basho is merely a polemic figure. But because Bond has a deep admiration for Shakespeare's "intellectual strength and passionate beauty," while rejecting as dishonest his solutions and, in particular, "the reconciliation that he created on the stage. . . ,"[40] *Bingo* raises serious questions.

Bond presents an irreconcilable conflict between the call for sanity and justice in Shakespeare's art, and the active complicity in an unjust, irrational society in Shakespeare's life. His Shakespeare becomes the type of artist who sells out morally, invalidates everything he writes because he separates art from life. In his next play, *The Fool,* Bond examines the counter-type: John Clare as a poet who refuses to compromise. But the ending is equally bleak because moral commitment is not enough. What Bond implies is that the artist has to have an ideological programme which he can use to change political institutions. Otherwise the pressures to conform to an irrational society, together with the outrage and frustration of his moral sense, will drive him mad. Here again Bond is paralleling contemporary German drama—in this case, Peter Weiss, whose play about *Hölderlin* (written four years before *The Fool*) deals with exactly the same subject: a

[39]Ibid., 24. Compare Bond's comment on *Narrow Road*: "What particularly incensed me about Basho was that everybody says, oh, what a marvellous poet. I think that is absolutely phoney. I mean that is bad poetry, that's academic phoney poetry. ... He says for instance that you get enlightenment where you are ... and everybody says, oh, how profound. People like Basho never get enlightenment where they are, because ... enlightenment should have come in the first scene of the play where he found the child" (Ibid., 9).

[40]Bond, *Plays: Two,* pp. ix and x.

proto-Marxist poet without a revolution who is driven mad by the irrationality he increasingly perceives around him. The moral—explicit in Weiss, implicit in Bond—seems to be that any truly ethical poet will be forced to withdraw into a cataleptic fugue without the benefit of Marx.

These poet-protagonists are clear reflections of Bond's changing perception of his role as a playwright. In his early plays, what is important is to free the individual from social repression. Any solution in the form of a political programme is seen as simply an alternative structure of coercion, which is the reason why Arthur's apotheosis at the end of *Early Morning* is a parody of Christ's ascension. At this stage, Bond rejects leaders along with uniforms and flag-poles, and in 1969 he declared: "No, I've no Utopia, no image of the society I want to see emerge. It would simply be people being themselves."[41] For Bond, the difference between Communism and Western democracy is only that between Shogo (who socializes his citizens by naked force) and Georgina (with her subtler but more insidious psychological intimidation). In 1970, he commented that "there is *no* viable political system in existence in the world at this moment . . ." (my italics); and in *Lear,* not only the old King and his monstrous daughters with their palace revolution, but also Cordelia and her peasant revolutionaries are all equally corrupted by the necessities of power.[42] Those who overthrow the system by violence perpetuate it, and even preaching a clearly defined political vision will create precisely the oppression it is designed to avoid. "We do not need a plan of the future, we need a *method* of change."[43]

But while working through this dilemma of ends and means in *Bingo,* Bond sets Shakespeare up as the representative of his own earlier viewpoint, which was that " 'you can change the world simply by being rational' . . ."—and shows that this attitude contributed to Shakespeare's suicide. As he commented: ". . . I wish that were true, but I don't think it is

---

[41]Bond, in *Observer,* 16 March 1969, p. 27.
[42]Bond and Hobson, 8. See also Scharine, p. 147.
[43]Bond, *Lear,* p. 11.

true. . . . [I]t is not possible to reach a rational world by wholly rational means. . . ."[44]

Of course Bond has already developed a basically irrational technique—the "aggro-effect"—though still in the hope of provoking rational thought and action outside the theatre. However, transferring this from the stage to politics is more than just a difference of degree. A therapeutic shock that jerks a deadened area of the individual's psyche back to life is one thing; a lobotomy, or the killing of some individuals for the good of others, however surgically this is done, is quite another. And when Bond advocates political violence (as in the misleadingly undated Author's Note in *Plays: One,* which was actually written in 1976 when he was working on *The Bundle*), then he is taking a position that his earlier plays have already convincingly shown to be untenable. In fact, the ending of *The Bundle* even denies what he had earlier declared "evident moral truths . . . things that are simply wrong in themselves. For example, it's evidently wrong to kill someone."[45] This reversal may be, as Bond has claimed, a measure of the urgency of the situation. But his arguments are not logically convincing. Either his rationale is one of *poetic* justice: "Class society must be violent, but it must also create the frustration, stimulation, aggression and . . . physical violence that are the means by which it can change into a classless society"; or, when he tries to define what legitimate violence is, he falls into the end-justifies-the-means fallacy: "Right-wing political violence cannot be justified because it always serves irrationality; but left-wing political violence is justified when it helps to create a more rational society. . . ."[46]

The contradictions in Bond's political position—as outlined in prefaces and essays which, almost by definition, are secondary to the plays—could perhaps be excused, since Bond is a playwright not a political scientist, if they were not reflected so directly in his stage work. But questions of politi-

---

[44]Edward Bond, "Conversation with Howard Davies," in Hay and Roberts, pp. 61–62.

[45]Bond and Asmus.

[46]Edward Bond, "On Violence," in *Plays: One,* pp. 14 and 17.

cal morality aside, the dramatic implications of Bond's acceptance of the commonplace argument for terrorist violence can be clearly seen in a play like *The Woman*. Here, in Bond's most ambitious play to date, we are given a summation of all his major thematic points. War is explicitly presented as both the product of class society and that society's way of perpetuating itself. War is absurd since "even victory would cost . . . more . . . than defeat at the beginning." The Statue of Good Fortune, for which the Trojan War is being fought in Bond's symbolic version of history, stands for the myths that legitimate an unjust society and trap or destroy the oppressors who rule through them even more than those they exploit. Arthur's madness, leading him to believe that a leader who kills everyone is the greatest benefactor, recurs in Hecuba's son; Arthur's parodic ascension is repeated by Hecuba in an even more grotesque form, as she is uplifted by a waterspout that "ripped out her hair and her eyes. Her tits were sticking up like knives."[47] In addition to Bond's image of socialization destroying the psyche in the murder of a child, we are shown the physical crippling of a slave as a symbol for the deformation of man to fit him for a biologically inappropriate role in technological society. Again a morally sane person, Ismene, who calls on the Greek soldiers to rebel because their officers are only using the war to enslave them, is driven mad by irrationality.

But here the situation is given an explicit solution: political violence and the natural life of a pastoral island. As Bond wrote in a letter to Tony Coult, "We mustn't write only problem plays, we must write answer plays. . . ."[48] The difficulty is the cliché nature of Bond's positive programme, which becomes expressed in an easiness of achievement that is dramatically unjustified. For the crippled slave to win a race against Heros, who is all that his name implies, demands a deliberate mystification of the audience. A man who is capable of transforming Athens into a tyranny with himself at the top, and

[47]Edward Bond, *The Woman* (London, 1979), pp. 108, etc.
[48]Edward Bond, "Letter to Tony Coult," 28 July 1977, in Hay and Roberts, p. 75.

who succumbs to such religious idealism that he orders his guards to throw away their weapons, is credible only on a purely symbolic level. Nothing we have seen of the Greek soldiers prepares us for an ending in which they are so dispirited by the death of their leader that they simply leave without any acts of revenge. In addition to this obvious manipulation of the dramatic action, Bond even has to stretch the logic of his symbols to make the play prove what he intends. The slave's deformed body stands explicitly for the effect of social repression which works on the mental level. In all Bond's other plays, the physical represents the psychological and emotional crippling, yet here the slave's moral sense, articulacy and kindness remain untouched by his upbringing and exploitation. Bond's source was Euripides' *Trojan Women,* and his title-change to *The Woman* is an indication of the play's thematic simplification. It is men who set up the repressive structures of a violent society, while (*pace* Victoria, Georgina, Bodice, Fontanelle, et al.) women keep their maternal instinct and so have the capacity to reject irrationality.

As Bond has put it, his first series ended with *The Sea,* which was "meant to *reassure* the audience they can cope with the problems dealt with in the series. . . ." His "second series ends with a *rhapsody,* which is in praise of human beings. In it right triumphs over bad. . . ." In structure as well as intention, it uses a contrast of "the carnage and waste of war" to "[*celebrate*] human tenacity and insight."[49] Despite a superficial similarity, there is a real difference in kind between reassurance and celebration. Similarly, "rhapsody," with its overtones of "enthusiastic extravagance," "emotionalism" and "wish-fulfillment"—qualities indeed reflected in the final positive state of *The Woman,* the Golden World of peasant innocence that is not only a somewhat impractical alternative to the modern situation, but one that had already been dismissed as illusory escapism in *Lear*—has very different connotations from the qualities of "analysis" or "social realism" which Bond stressed in his earlier plays.

If politics were indeed all, it would be comparatively easy

---

[49]Bond and Innes, 108; my italics.

to evaluate this development in Bond's work. When answers are so simplistic, serious doubt must be cast on the way the questions have been formulated. And since Bond's didacticism determines the shape of his drama, if his attack on society is discredited, then his message would seem to invalidate his plays. Yet, in fact, any critic dealing with Bond comes up against a conflict between means and ends similar to the dichotomy that Bond himself addresses within his work, since his plays defy easy categories. Apart from Shaw and Brecht, no other twentieth-century dramatist has deliberately measured himself against the standard of Shakespeare. The politics that make his work flawed are also what give it such moral force that it demands to be taken seriously. He is the only English-speaking dramatist who has managed to build significantly on Brecht, and his plays have had at least one tangible political effect—the abolition of censorship in the English theatre—even if the victory was an easy one by that time, since such plays as Osborne's *A Patriot for Me* had already revealed how anachronistic the Lord Chamberlain's powers were. Still, what other contemporary playwright could so legitimately claim, as Bond did in discussing *The Woman,* to have actually fulfilled the "need to set our scenes in public places, where history is formed, classes clash and whole societies move. Otherwise we're not writing about the events that most affect us and shape our future."[50]

[50]Bond, "Green Room," 8.

David Hare

by Colin Ludlow

In [an] . . . interview on television, David Hare declared
that he is not a social doctor prescribing remedies for our
national ills. Nevertheless, like most dramatists of his generation, he is concerned with diagnosing our social condition.
The particular interest and originality of his plays lies in the
immense variety of subject matter and styles he employs to
illuminate that condition. In *Teeth 'n' Smiles,* he uses a rock
band playing at a Cambridge May Ball as a framework for
wider comment. In *Knuckle,* he adopts a thriller format. *Fanshen* tells the story of the Chinese revolution in a particular
village employing a Brechtian narrative style. *Brassneck,* which
he wrote with Howard Brenton, is an exuberant sweep
through post-war British history, exposing the corruption
and political in-fighting in an imaginary Midlands town. The
effectiveness with which he handles these different styles and
subjects reveals his considerable talent as a writer.

Hare's play . . . *Plenty* . . . opened at the National Theatre
in April [1978]. It is a compelling study of a girl who serves
during the war as an agent in France, and then returns to
Britain afterwards to experience disillusion and despair. The
history of Susan Traherne is traced through some twenty
years. In that time, she is unable to find work she can believe
in, she fails to become pregnant when she desires a child. She
slips into marriage, but has decidedly ambivalent feelings
towards her diplomat husband, and finally leaves him. The
play is written with Hare's customary sharpness and wit, but

the wit exposes suffering, it does not undercut it. In one devastating scene, set at the time of Suez, Susan and her husband entertain a senior diplomat, Sir Leonard Darwin, at their home in Knightsbridge. Susan's conversation is barbed with witty and scathing remarks which reveal, not a taste for drawing room humour, but genuine anguish and indignation at what has happened. There is more naked pain in *Plenty* than in any of Hare's previous work, and that pain [was] burningly portrayed by Kate Nelligan, who [gave] an inspired performance as Susan.

In his second full-length play, *The Great Exhibition,* Hare consciously parodies what he sees as the typical Royal Court play emphasizing characters who suffer. The plot is shamelessly lifted from *Look Back in Anger*: Charlie Hammett, a middle-class Labour MP, has an affair with his upper-class wife's best friend after his wife leaves him. However, the anguish of the characters involved in these events is not taken particularly seriously. Rather it is presented as self-indulgence and vigorously mocked. It is indicative of Hare's development therefore that if one seeks for parallels to *Plenty, Look Back in Anger* immediately springs to mind. Susan is no latter-day Jimmy Porter, mowing down all that she encounters with her rhetoric, nor has *Plenty* any of the sentimental romanticism found in Osborne's play. But both plays are rooted in the disappointed hopes of the immediate post-war years, in the pain of individuals who long for change but find it unforthcoming.

At the beginning of the final scene of *Plenty,* a dark hotel room suddenly separates like a curtain to reveal the green fields of France bathed in glorious sunshine on the day of liberation. It is a striking visual image for the dawn of a new age, and Susan's final words as she happily surveys this scene are "There will be days and days and days like this." They are heavy with irony, for the play has already shown the falseness of that dawn, the dampening of that joy. By relating Susan's experience to major historical events, Hare is able to suggest that her disillusion is representative rather than merely individual, and thus the play becomes a form of social commentary as it examines the general as well as the particular causes of Susan's problem.

The chief target for attack is not however the entire social and political system, it is the British characteristic of emotional reserve, the repression of feelings. Sir Leonard Darwin is afforded a certain respect in the play, because, however out-dated his reasons, he expresses his outrage at the time of Suez over the government's failure to keep the Civil Service in-formed. It is the common lack of such courage, the general refusal to give vent to one's feelings and speak one's mind, that is implicitly suggested to be the cause of the stagnation in society which is at the root of Susan's pain. Susan herself, though quite prepared to let go and certainly not lacking the courage of her convictions, is nevertheless inhibited because there is nowhere she can direct her energy when surrounded by people who stoically accept their situation. As she herself remarks, "I'd like to change everything but I don't know how."

As a play for Britain in the late 'seventies, *Plenty* is perhaps limited by Hare's choice of subject matter. Though frustration at the absence of change may still be rife, the play is so firmly located in the disappointment of hopes aroused by the end of the war that it lacks immediacy to our present situation. The play feels historical rather than absolutely contemporary. Nevertheless, on the whole is succeeds because the character of Susan is powerfully and convincingly drawn, and because its broader social implications are neither laboured nor over-stressed. It throws out provoking suggestions about the na-ture and problems of our society, but it does not reduce the complexity of these questions either by trying to pass off the story of one girl as an encapsulation of the entire situation, or by proposing facile solutions.

The lack of stridency in *Plenty*, its implicit rather than overtly argued social comment, have led some critics to con-clude that it lacks substance and has nothing to say. This is pure laziness on their behalf, but it demonstrates the extent to which Hare refuses to prescribe cures for the problems he highlights. His plays are refreshingly understated for modern social and political drama. They cannot be reduced to a simple message, for his characters are not manipulated simply to prove a thesis. The power of his work is to provoke thought and disturb complacency. Certainly the study of suffering and waste in *Plenty* does no less than that.

Adultery Is Next to Godlessness: Dramatic Juxtaposition in Peter Nichols's *Passion Play*

by June Schlueter

[In the late 1970's,] the London theatre . . . experienced a diffusion of the intense politicism that characterized its fringe in the late 1960's and early 1970's. Though the same generation of playwrights remains the lifeblood of the contemporary stage and politics are often its concern, the political spine that gave structure to the theatre of a decade ago has splintered into sinews of dramatic subjects, not the least of which is sex. Yet while those playwrights who favor sexual politics over just-plain politics have a ready market in both London and New York, some of the most dramatically interesting plays have come from those who have transcended the Neil Simon version of sex that has dominated the contemporary theatre. Harold Pinter, for example, would seem an unlikely reviver of the "eternal triangle," yet this veteran British playwright turned a play about adultery into one of the conversation pieces of the seventies. *Betrayal,* which dramatizes in reverse the nine-year love affair of a man with his best friend's wife, suggests the formal challenge of the contemporary playwright who sees sex as a legitimate dramatic subject but is unprepared to reduce it to a Simonesque smirk or a class in Fellatio 101.

One of the more technically ambitious treatments of

"Adultery Is Next to Godlessness: Dramatic Juxtaposition in Peter Nichols's *Passion Play*." From June Schlueter, "Adultery Is Next to Godlessness: Dramatic Juxtaposition in Peter Nichols's *Passion Play*," *Modern Drama,* XXIV, 4(1981), 540–5. Copyright © 1981 by the University of Toronto. Reprinted by permission.

adultery in recent years is Peter Nichols's *Passion Play*, which opened in London in January of 1981. Like the subject of Pinter's *Betrayal,* that of *Passion Play* is infidelity, between husband and wife and between friends. James Croxley has been married to Eleanor for twenty-five years, during which time there have been no sexual transgressions on his part. But Kate, who is rebounding from an affair with the recently deceased Albert, finds James attractive and begins the seduction that will culminate in the affair, the discovery, and the ultimatum. Intimacies multiply as James learns that Eleanor also had an affair with Albert, and Eleanor and Albert's wife, Agnes, make the women who have betrayed them their confidantes. Though the situation is the standard fare of sexual comedy, Nichols's strategic use of dramatic juxtaposition offers a perspective of faith and infidelity that an audience seasoned to on- and off-stage adultery does not expect. By the end of the play, it is clear that adultery is Nichols's metaphor for the essential emptiness of a godless world.

The most unusual dramatic device that Nichols uses is that of the double character/actor, through which Jim materializes as James's alter ego and Nell as Eleanor's, enabling the audience to know the thoughts of the central characters while others on stage do not. Though London *Times* reviewer Irving Wardle expressed amazement that no one had employed such dramatic doubles before,[1] both Eugene O'Neill and Brian Friel have, of course, done so. O'Neill, in *Days Without End* (1932), dramatizes the moral division between "John," representing the good half of the self, and "Loving," representing the evil, splitting his central character into warring halves in a battle over religious faith. Similarly, Friel, in *Philadelphia, Here I Come!* (1964), employs two actors, one designated "Public" and the other "Private," to examine the emotional conflict of his central character, Gareth O'Donnell, on the eve of his departure for America. Nichols's creation of the double character, like those of O'Neill and Friel, suggests the dramatist's attempt to get be-

[1] Irving Wardle, "Doing Justice to the Theme of Adultery: *Passion Play,*" *The Times* (London), 14 January 1981, p. 11.

neath the surface of the characters to the subtext, where the intentions that impel action reside. But in Nichols's play, Jim and Nell not only illuminate the characters of James and Eleanor, but acquire lives of their own, turning the subtext of the play into the central action.

Although there is little incompatibility of character between James and Jim (they work together admirably well), Jim turns out to be the more interesting of the two. The alter ego of the man who beds both wife and mistress appears on the scene the moment that James's deception begins. Having returned home from lunch with Kate, James is uncertain about what to tell Eleanor, until Jim materializes to fabricate the excuse. The juxtaposition of the two male characters ranges from comic to pathetic, as Jim consistently proves to be quicker on the uptake than James and somewhat wiser in his perceptions, though no less impulsive in his deeds. Jim, for example, telephones Kate while James is still making amends with his wife, and though Jim recognizes the folly in complying with Kate's request for a love letter, he enthusiastically assists James in composing one.

Eleanor's alter ego, Nell, appears in a tearoom scene in which Agnes enlightens Eleanor about her husband's infidelity. Still vengeful over Kate's live-in affair with Albert, Agnes has been appropriating the younger woman's mail, and she now possesses the love letter James wrote. Nichols intercuts the women's dialogue with a conversation between James and Jim, who are glowing in the resurgence of life Kate has brought them. At the same moment that Agnes hands over the incriminating letter to Eleanor, James stamps the envelope containing it, unaware that his scribblings of passion will be rerouted to his wife. As Eleanor receives the letter, her alter ego appears, sits between the two women, and reads: " 'Of course I'm longing to be in your bed again but there aren't many chances to leave the house. . . . I liked it when you spilt wine from your mouth into mine. . . .' "[2]

But the comic effect of Nichols's masterful dramatic jux-

[2]Peter Nichols, *Passion Play* (London, 1981), p. 44. Subsequent citations will be given parenthetically in the text.

tapositions in this scene is tempered by the sharp division in the characters of Eleanor and Nell, who are not the conspiring team that James and Jim are. In the former case, Eleanor is clearly the social mask the character stubbornly retains, while Nell is the distressed woman behind it: Eleanor continues her conversations with Agnes with tearoom civility, while Nell screams out her humiliation and rage.

The subdrama begun by Nell becomes even more compelling in the confrontation scene that follows, in which all four marital partners are present. In that scene, Eleanor returns home to find James just completing a telephone call with Kate. She responds to her husband's greeting with silence, leaving James and Jim to puzzle over her mood and to wonder how much she knows. Whereas Eleanor says nothing, however, Nell is especially loquacious, vigorously interrogating and attacking James with questions and accusations only the audience can hear. When Eleanor presents James with the written evidence, Nell's expressions of bitterness alternate with Jim's confessions of relief at having been discovered. But the most appealing part of the subdrama, which becomes crucial to the moral life of the play, is that Eleanor and Nell themselves have transgressed, and they now use this information to gain psychological advantage. With James's infidelity disclosed, Eleanor reveals one of her own, with Albert. But Nell reveals yet another, which only the audience hears: years earlier, she had had an affair with a man for whom she nearly left James. In the network of infidelities, then, Eleanor cannot trust James, James cannot trust Eleanor, neither Eleanor nor James can trust Kate, Kate cannot trust Agnes, and Agnes can trust neither Eleanor nor Kate.

As Act I ends, Jim is busy planning his strategy for continuing the affair with Kate that James promised Eleanor he would end. Wardle, arguing in his review of the London production that the play should have stopped there, contends that the "essential statement has already been made, . . ." and that in Act II Nichols could only repeat it.[3] But the situation at the end of Act II is not identical to that of Act I, for as the

[3]Wardle, p. 11.

interplay between the characters and their alter egos and between Jim and Nell confirms, the subtext now dominates the play. Dramatically and psychologically, the alter egos are far more interesting in the second act than Eleanor and James, who themselves become minor characters as Jim and Nell acquire autonomy. In Act II, Jim quarrels with Eleanor over her suspicions, Nell confides in Agnes, and Jim and Nell carry on a conversation that is independent of their public counterparts.

Nell, of course, has been developing as the most complex and dramatically effective character of the four. Jim, it turns out, is every bit as indifferent morally to his marital commitment as James is, and as the play continues, the audience understands increasingly that Jim is simply the mirror image of James, for whom there is no disparity between behavior and thought. Jim is more appealing only because he is more capable in his cunning, but he reveals nothing to which James's behavior and language do not already attest. Nell, on the other hand, behaves in ways that are completely uncharacteristic of Eleanor. When Eleanor discovers that her husband and Kate are still involved with each other, Nell expresses the almost unendurable humiliation of having misplaced her trust in husband and friend for a second time. It is Nell, not Eleanor, who turns to Agnes to speak of her stupidity in not having been able to read the signs of the infidelity. In a scene that takes place over Kate's laundry, which Eleanor has offered to wash, Nell attacks Jim "with her fists, pounding at his chest and shoulders"; when he collapses, "she kicks at him with her bare feet" (p. 97). And, finally, it is Nell, not Eleanor, who visits a psychiatrist, overdoses on sleeping pills, packs her bag, and leaves, as Eleanor and James go through the motions of a domestic Christmas scene.

But the second part of Nichols's play is essential also because it clarifies the major juxtaposition of the play: that of James's sexual passion with the Christian Passion. Act II opens with the chorale "O Haupt voll Blut und Wunden" from Bach's *St. Matthew Passion.* If we recall James's letter to Kate— " 'Of course I'm longing to be in your bed again but there aren't many chances to leave the house. Later this year there's

the Matthew Passion and towards Christmas Messiah and the
Verdi Requiem ...'" (p. 44)—we may infer that several
months have passed since the discovery. James, who is a re-
storer of modern paintings, is at work on a Victorian crucifix,
and Eleanor is preparing her part in the *St. Matthew Passion.*
The scene is crucial to the play, for in it James speaks of the
connection between religion and sex that Nichols has been
implying throughout Act I.

Events in that act are repeatedly juxtaposed with strains
of the Mozart *Requiem.* When Kate first sends her message to
James, for example, by telling Eleanor she finds him attractive, the "Dies Irae" bursts upon the stage:

> Day of wrath, that day dismaying,
> Shall fulfill the prophets' saying,
> Earth in smouldering ashes laying.
> Oh, how great the dread, the sighing,
> When the Judge, the All-descrying,
> Shall appear, all secrets trying.

The association of the Passion of Jesus Christ with the passion
of James Croxley (the etymological similarity between Croxley
and cross is immediately apparent, as are the J.C. initials)
becomes explicit during the first sexual encounter between
James and Kate. In that scene, the "Agnus Dei," the last
movement of the *Requiem,* which prays that the Lamb of God
grant everlasting peace to the dead, becomes, in a practical
sense, the measure of their sexual affair. As James caresses
Kate on the sofa, he listens to the live radio broadcast in which
Eleanor takes part: "This is the 'Agnus Dei.' I'll have to be
going soon. There's only the 'Lux Perpetua' and the 'Cum
Sanctis Tuis' to come" (p. 24). As the fugue swells and fades,
James hastens out the door, hoping to arrive home before
Eleanor. He succeeds this time, but by the end of Act I,
Eleanor has discovered the betrayal. Fulfilling the prophecy
of the "Dies Irae," the wronged woman gives James the ulti-
matum, as strains of "Quam Elim Abraham" from the
"Domine" resound: "Deliver the souls of all the faithful dead
from the punishment of hell. ..."

Paradoxically, the *Requiem* is a source of humor in Act I,

offering the audience the delight of recognizing the pun on "passion" and the incongruity of juxtaposing the solemnity of Christ's suffering on the Cross with the triviality of James Croxley's indulgence. Yet the thematic connection between the two becomes significant in this opening scene of Act II, as James asks Eleanor, "What does all that mean? What's it all about?," and Eleanor replies: "head full of blood and wounds, full of sorrow and scoffing. Mocked with a crown of thorns. . . ." The sense of suffering and sorrow, of mockery and scorn, conveyed by Bach's *Passion* characterizes the relationship between the couple in Act II, which, like the Victorian crucifix on which James was working, cannot be restored. "Gave it up," he announces, and then explains why:

> I'd had enough of that insipid eunuch. We still live in the shadow of His death. And His birth too, for that matter. A virgin birth. A conception and a birth without carnal love. It flies in the face of all we know and people like us don't believe it any more. But we can't forget two thousand years of it in a hurry.   (p. 60)

If Nichols has been hinting all along of the connection between the Passion of Christ and James's passion, James makes the connection explicit by recognizing in the Victorian painting a perverted attempt on the part of Christianity to make the language of sexual passion its own:

> even sexual passion is twisted into a craving for the infinite. The anti-lifers, the troubadours, the saints and martyrs. Saint Teresa caught by Bernini mid-orgasm, pierced by the lance of God. Anyone who's ever watched a partner in the act can see that's a statue of a woman coming. She's in ecstasy. The Christians took over the language of sexual emotion for their own purposes— passion, love, adoration, ecstasy, . . . those words are now more meaningless than the so-called dirty words. All spoilt, one way or another. So that we can't even talk about it any more.   (p. 60)

James would have his sex free of Christianity and hence free of monogamy: "before the church took over, people used to make love in crowds. Before the god-lovers and life-haters set down 'The Couple' as the largest legitimate sexual group" (p. 61).

As Nell explains to her psychiatrist, James sees Christianity as "a terrible disaster forced on the rest of us by madmen in the Middle Ages" (p. 79). For James, Kate, who is young, unconventional, and independent, can be their salvation: "She parks on double yellow lines, she walks straight to the head of the queues, she grabs what's going—." "In other words," Eleanor replies, "disregards the morality you've always lived by." "We need her, Eleanor," he insists, "she can save us" (pp. 94, 95). But Kate's loveless passion is a younger generation's perversion of the Passion of Christianity, which James can only define as "Suffering. Self-inflicted torture. Masochism. All that's holy" (p. 83).

Though Nell does not have the perspective or the emotional resources to understand, she speaks to her psychiatrist about the "sudden black abyss" of her life, about the sense of community she felt in church as a child, though she never believed in God, and about James's attitude toward her visits:

> He doesn't like me seeing you. It smacks of the Church, he says, employing a professional to listen to our secrets. It means we've lost faith in human intercourse. Two godless people using a third who neither knows nor cares about them but who can blame or let them off, according to some rules made long ago by someone else.
> (p. 79)

As the strains of the *St. Matthew Passion* give way to blaring rock music and the Victorian crucifix is replaced by an abstract study in yellow, it becomes clear that Nell cannot find redemption in a world in which only the forms of religion and marriage prevail.

In the past decade, a host of modern British plays have affirmed that there are a limited number of dramatic variations on the theme of adultery, all of which have worn thin. Yet *Passion Play* succeeds not only in treating adultery on the contemporary stage but in examining the failures of a contemporary life in which, as Agnes tells Nell, "Faith is a luxury you can't afford now. Or even again" (p. 86). Through skillful dramatic juxtaposition of characters, scenes, and passions, Nichols has turned adultery into both a manifestation and a metaphor of a faithless world.

The Politics of Anxiety: Contemporary Socialist Theatre in England

by C. W. E. Bigsby

[The year 1981 saw] a number of somewhat subdued celebrations of the twenty-fifth anniversary of the Royal Court Theatre in its present form, and of John Osborne's play *Look Back in Anger*. Celebration is not without its ironies, since in many ways the mood and style of the fifties are staging a come-back. History repeats itself, this time, perhaps, as farce. Whereas Sir Harold Macmillan had told the British that they had never had it so good, Mrs. Margaret Thatcher now tells them that they have had it far too good for far too long. But both periods are characterized by the disintegration of old models of behaviour and national purpose. There is a sense now as then of cultural crisis. Then it was Suez; now it is economic decline. And for twenty-five years we have had a theatre which has acknowledged this sense of unease, instability, usually in social or political terms, but in the case of writers like Harold Pinter, Joe Orton and Tom Stoppard, at least, in terms which raise ontological and epistemological questions. Indeed, even those writers initially hailed as representing some kind of breakthrough on a social or political level were in fact responding to a more profound sense of dislocation than could be contained by such an analysis.

The late fifties have for long been presented as a breakthrough for a new socially committed drama which engaged

"The Politics of Anxiety: Contemporary Socialist Theatre in England." From C. W. E. Bigsby, "The Politics of Anxiety: Contemporary Socialist Theatre in England," *Modern Drama*, XXIV, 4 (1981), 393–403. Copyright © 1981 by the University of Toronto. Reprinted by permission.

the problems of the working class and entertained the novel thought that life survived outside London. This mythicising was from the start an acknowledgement of the fact that the English theatre had traditionally reflected, in its writers, directors and plays, the values of a particular section of English society, most major writers sharing an educational and class background which to some degree shaped or influenced their work. In this context the new theatre in Britain seemed socially revolutionary, if in some ways theatrically regressive. The emergence of a number of writers whose class origins were different from those of their predecessors created the impression of a radical disjunction, of a theatre concerned with addressing itself to social realities, to the experiences of those displaced from theatrical no less than political concern. Their plays were seen as parallels to such novels as *Saturday Night and Sunday Morning, Room at the Top* and *This Sporting Life*.

But in fact Osborne's plays, for example, are addressed to more than the collapse of imperial pretensions and shifts in the social system. Stoppard may have sought to intensify the metaphysical implications of Archie Rice's line in Osborne's second play, *The Entertainer* ("Don't clap, it's a very old building"), by having one of his characters in *Rosencrantz and Guildenstern Are Dead* remark, "Don't clap, it's a very old world," yet actually that metaphysical dimension was always there. The social order, character, language, are all shown in a state of disrepair. The familiar structures no longer locate the individual in a reassuring world. The stage (here the music-hall stage, as for Stoppard, later, it would be the Shakespearian stage) becomes an image not only of the desperate fictions acted out with diminishing confidence by the politicians of late-fifties Britain, but of the role-playing of individuals cut adrift from the history they had assumed to be the origin of their private significance. The Anglo-French invasion of Suez was not merely a political watershed; it was one more evidence of a collapse which went beyond the social, and which surfaces in Osborne's work as a generalised sense of bafflement, in particular, in the image of the disintegrating figure of Archie

Rice, no longer able to sustain his role, his identity or his language.

Arnold Wesker, too, presented as a socialist playwright, and seeing himself in those terms, was struck by the failure of his own times to conform to the ideological neatness of pre-war battles between fascism and progressive forces. In *Chicken Soup with Barley,* he projects his characters into that past, as many of the socialist playwrights of the seventies were to do. But for the most part, his characters are shown struggling to locate themselves in an uncertain world, anxious to defend themselves against a form of alienation expressed through, but not originating in, class divisions. Despite the implied confidence in an emerging personal and class identity, in reality his plays tend to undermine their own premises. In fact his work has always been infiltrated by profound pessimism, perhaps at its most obvious in the early *Chips with Everything* and *Their Very Own and Golden City.* His plays incline to be concerned with a struggle towards articulateness which is presented ostensibly as synonymous with emerging selfhood and awakened class vigour; but this tends to be balanced by an awareness of the deadening power of inertia and, more significantly, by a suspicion of that articulateness which may be nothing more than the displacement of a sense of social and psychological impotence. Hence Beatie, in *Roots,* achieves a fluency which we have already learned to distrust in the character of Ronnie, her errant and, as it turns out, treacherous lover. This suspicion is voiced later in *The Journalists,* and though *The Old Ones* seems to endorse the need to sound the authentic note of the self, that self has spent a lifetime trapped in the dead language of others, and is fragile to the point of irony.

As for Pinter, his class origins were, of course, a red herring from the start. His working-class characters have never been designed to serve political or social objectives. In his hands, class becomes simply one more ironic tool, one more evidence of the gap between language and referent, the real and the imagined, the desired and the actual.

But if the decade which followed 1956 was not quite what

it appeared to be, 1968 did see the birth of a genuine socialist theatre, though within a decade this too had been infiltrated by a degree of doubt which turned ideological assurance into ontological insecurity. For the moment, however, and for a new generation of writers, the convulsions of 1968 marked the possibility of a radical shift in national and international politics, the stirrings of a new radicalism which demanded a dramatic response. It became easier to address immediate political issues directly with the abolition, in the same year, of theatre censorship.

Paradoxically, despite their commitment to engaging the present, a large number of socialist plays have been set, in fact, in the past, partly because they could thereby dramatise ideological conflicts more clearly without the interference patterns generated by a pragmatic socialist government and a welfare state which, as Iris Murdoch has argued, tends to drain English politics of ideological theory and purposive action. And they were set in the past partly because the true subject of revolution is history. That is, they were inclined to endorse E. M. Carr's conviction that history is a dialogue between events of the past and progressively emerging future ends. Hence, when John Arden wrote *The Non-Stop Connolly Show,* when Caryl Churchill wrote *A Light Shining in Buckinghamshire,* or David Hare *Fanshen,* or Steve Gooch *The Women Pirates,* or John McGrath *The Cheviot, The Stag and the Black, Black Oil,* or Edward Bond *Bingo,* and so on, their efforts did not mean that England was necessarily experiencing a sudden interest in historical drama. Rather, they suggest that history is offered as a clue to the present, that theirs is offered as a drama of praxis. Nonetheless, it is worth remarking that in times of stress and confusion the past is an attractive place to hide. But of course not even the past is secure if it is in the hands of others—something which is clear enough to black writers and historians in America and Africa, as to those who live in countries where the encyclopaedias are liable to sudden and arbitrary revision. It is not for nothing that the Poles have a saying that "the hardest thing to predict is the past."

1968 was an ambiguous phenomenon in England. Its

ideological component was by no means clear. Nonetheless, events had a considerable impact on individual writers, in particular on John Arden, John McGrath, Howard Brenton, David Hare and David Edgar, several of whom encountered the events of 1968 elsewhere—in France and in America. 1968 also marked the first stirrings of a feminist theatre movement which did not really get into its stride until the mid-seventies with the founding of the Women's Theatre Group in 1975 and Monstrous Regiment in 1976.

1968 also marked the beginnings of the theatrical fringe in London, sparked in part by a number of expatriate Americans, from the "libertarian anarchist" Jim Haynes, who founded the Arts Lab (which in turn inspired a number of other groups, like the Portable Theatre, Freehold and the People Show), through Charles Marowitz and Ed Berman, to Nancy Meckler and Beth Porter, from La Mama, who founded the Freehold Company. In 1965 the Cartoon Archetypical Slogan Theatre had been founded, the first of a growing number of socialist theatre groups which eventually expanded to include Welfare State (1968), 7:84 (1971), Hull Truck (1971), Red Ladder (1973), Belt and Braces (1973), and many others. As the title of one of them suggests—the Agitprop Street Players (1968)—these tended at first to dramatise immediate issues in agitprop form.

The 7:84 company, founded by John McGrath, created a distinctive style which involves music, dialogue, broad humour and caustic satire. This theatre grows out of dramaturgy—at its best in McGrath's own *Little Red Hen,* a dramatic kaleidoscope of Scottish working-class history, or in *Yobbo Nowt,* an account of the emerging authority of a working-class woman, told in song and brief sketches—which aims to educate, to raise consciousness, to demonstrate a vitality which is itself offered as a principal resource in the battle against capitalism. It mocks its own aesthetic pretensions and resists generating works which can be seen as mere artifacts, the playwrights being aware of the risk of deflecting attention from content to form—a problem identified by John Arden in *The Non-Stop Connolly Show,* in which he actually has a character denounce Connolly for his failure to make this distinction, for his substitution of emotional response for rational analysis.

This theatre makes directness of style and analysis a primary virtue. Indeed, directness is one of the prime virtues listed by McGrath in his descriptive definition of committed socialist art. Though individual characters may invent a code behind which to hide their true intentions and desires, that cipher is broken by the processes of the play which can conceive of no effect without cause, no mystery resistant to rationality, no current of human nature or the human condition with the power to sweep aside the implacable and revelatory facts of history. Indeed, to David Hare and David Edgar it was precisely the theatre's power to penetrate the lie which made it the ideal tool for the socialist writer.

Of course, this is also the logic behind the devices employed by Erwin Piscator and Bertolt Brecht: the printed slogans, the still and moving films, which are designed to ensure that a scene has been completely drained of any meaning which exists to be apprehended moment by moment. When these devices are most effective, the consequence in dramatic terms is directness of effect, a raw power which derives from the total release of energy, that total release being its primary function and method. The subversive view of historical process, after all, has its own *frisson*. The audience is offered the flattering role of appearing as the cutting edge of history, the culmination of historic process. And because the central assumption of such work is the essentially shared experience of deprivation, this drama offers that communal experience, that sense of participating in a theatrical event, which could itself be, as the American theatre of the sixties showed, a powerful and transforming sensation. Theatre becomes an epiphany. It asserts a continuity between the theatrical experience and the social world which is not simply the somewhat mystical one claimed by Peter Brook and Jerzy Grotowski, but an engagement with the immediate: in some degree the theatre is an image of that communal experience which it claims as its subject.

But at its worst this committed theatre allows itself to be

too fully known. Character defers to role, the anguished self to class function, the ambiguities of human motives and the confused facts of action—half-willed, half-contingent—to a clear-minded rational response to a world in which nothing remains hidden. It is, in other words, the unreality of its realism which threatens its truth. And this is a view which David Edgar and David Hare in particular seem eventually to have endorsed.

The paradox is that while these plays are aesthetically open—assuming a permeable membrane between audience and performer, inviting the involvement and commitment of the working-class audience to whom they are addressed—many of them remain ideologically closed. They begin with their conclusions. Jean-Paul Sartre once attacked the French Communist Party for its tendency to evade debate by the simple procedure of discrediting opponents as "fascists." In this context, Edward Bond's description of Tom Stoppard as a fascist betokens nothing so much as an evasion. More generally, the strategy in many of these plays which turns kings into simple betrayers, captains of slave-ships into cynical manipulators *only,* judges into conscious dealers in injustice *and nothing else*—this tactic is borrowed from the forces these dramas would engage. Insofar as this theatre not only assaults historic injustice and inveterate class diabolism, but also adopts the reductive process whereby entire classes are dismissed as wholly knowable and hence wholly ignorable, it becomes guilty of similar offences. Consequently, although David Edgar would not choose to disavow this period of his work, he has come to feel that a primary weakness of agitprop lies in the fact that it underestimates the power and sophistication of the forces it would indict, that it fails to acknowledge the ambiguity which may prove the primary reason for the failure of private and public visions.

Socialist theatre has also had to come to terms with political developments in England. After a period in the early seventies when working-class solidarity seemed to have the power to exercise real authority over national policies, and even to precipitate the collapse of a government, there followed first a socialist government forced to compromise on its central principles, and then the most reactionary government in recent British history. The interventional power of socialist theatre was evidently negligible. For writers like Hare, Edgar and Brenton, this situation raised questions about the adequacy of their stance, their effectiveness in locating an audience, the style which they employed and the authority of their plays. The result was a shift to the larger stages of the subsidised companies and to television—in search of a new and wider audience—and a shift to a more realistic mode. These playwrights changed direction in order to examine the alienation which they felt increasingly to lie behind problems that surfaced in the form of a political reaction or collapse of moral sensibility, but which originated at a level not susceptible of simplistic analysis. Their work has become more dense and more occluded. As well, it shows more concern with the point of intersection of private and public worlds, with the radical instability in experience, and with the plight of the individual who finds himself the focus of pressures which do not yield so easily to conscience or to ideological analysis.

To a degree, I suspect that the early plays of Hare, Edgar and Brenton, the work of the Portable Theatre and possibly of Belt and Braces and other such companies, were based on an assumption derived, perhaps, from early Brecht and from Piscator and Sergein Tretyakov: that an attack on illusionism, on naturalism, is already an assault on the bourgeoisie and the comfortable process of containment which it favours in art. They have all, to some degree or other, moved away from this stance while retaining elements of agtiprop in style, structure and characterisation, though others, like Howard Barker, have not made this move. They have not abandoned their socialism, but they have perhaps moved from what Walter Benjamin once called "the presence of the now" (a kind of compounding of past and present into an explosive force) to what he later called "tactics of attrition." But the fear, more and more, is that expressed in Brecht's poem, about Benjamin, in which he says: "Tactics of attrition are what you enjoyed / Sitting at the chess table in the pear tree's shade. / The enemy who drove you from your books / Will not be worn down by the likes of us."[1] Further, there is a dominating sense in much recent English socialist theatre of loss of direction, conviction, purpose—a fear that in the battle of attrition, it may not be the committed writer who survives. The irony is that in some ways it is this fact which has given the work of this theatre its power to penetrate beyond the fact to the image, beyond the word to the symbol. The alienation of David Hare's *Licking Hitler* and *Dreams of Leaving,* the acknowledged failure behind the apparent triumphs in David Edgar's *Mary Barnes* and *The Jail Diary of Albie Sachs,* the privatism of Howard Brenton's *Sore Throats,* the cold vision of unyielding blankness in Barrie Keeffee's *Gimme Shelter* and Stephen Poliakoff's *Bloody Kids,* have replaced the confident and energetic satire of the early seventies.

McGrath attacks such writers for their careerism. He is plainly wide of the mark. If anything, Edgar is more active on the political scene than he had been earlier in his career when he was content to let his plays do the work for him. It is rather that some confidence has been lost, not only in the nature of political development in the country but in the power of art to operate quite so directly in the modelling of character, history and language as these writers had earlier proposed with such a sense of conviction. The moral assurance remains—it provides the impulse for their work; but this work now bears the marks of pressure which is not merely social in origin, and it no longer views alienation as a pure product of history or of unreconstructed capitalism. Something of the same might be said of Bond, whose plays are almost invariably accompanied by prefaces which attempt to close the gaps left in the plays.

To some extent, the political earnestness has declined in the works of these writers, though not, for the most part, in their public statements. It has been replaced on the one hand by a greater concern for the ambiguities of experience, and on the other, perhaps, by a greater concern for the processes of

---

[1]Walter Benjamin, and Bertolt Brecht, "Ermattungstaktik," quoted in Stanley Mitchell, Introduction, *Understanding Brecht,* by Walter Benjamin (London, 1977), trans. Anya Bostock, pp. xvii–xviii.

theatre. In this, too, I am reminded of Brecht. He once said that he often dreamed of being interrogated by a tribunal that asked, " 'Now tell us, Mr. Brecht, are you really in earnest?' I would have to admit that no, I'm not completely in earnest. I think too much about artistic problems, you know, about what is good for the theatre, to be completely in earnest. But having said 'no' to that important question, I would add something still more important: namely, that my attitude is *permissible*."[2] I would prefer to say that Hare's and Edgar's attitudes are not merely permissible; they are in some sense desirable, even from the point of view of those who see the theatre as the necessary means of subverting authority on all levels. Indeed, an argument could be advanced that the more profoundly subversive text is not that work which challenges versions of history and exposes the mechanisms of power, but that which acknowledges the authoritarian power, the ideological force of language, the coercive strength of myth, and the social and metaphysical reassurance implicit in realism. As Theodor Adorno once observed, "Cultural conservatives who demand that a work of art should say something, join forces with their political opponents against atelic, hermetic works of art. Eulogists of 'relevance' are more likely to find Sartre's *Huis Clos* profound, than to listen patiently to a text whose language challenges signification and by its very distance from meaning revolts in advance against positivist subordination of meaning."[3] Seen in this way, of course, the truly subversive writer becomes not Arden but Orton, not McGrath but Pinter, not Gooch but Beckett. And Adorno advances precisely this argument, attempting to reconcile his Marxist stance with the reified position of post-modernism by insisting on the ineluctable realism of art. But in doing so, he already goes beyond the Marxist position in whose name he attempts this reconciliation. Thus he observes of Beckett: "Philosophical apologists may laud his works as sketches from an anthropology. But

[2]Bertolt Brecht, as quoted in Walter Benjamin, "Conversations with Brecht," trans. Anya Bostock, in Ernst Bloch, et al., *Aesthetics and Politics*, trans. ed. Ronald Taylor (London, 1980), p. 87.
[3]Theodor Adorno, "Commitment," trans. Francis McDonagh, in *Aesthetics and Politics*, p. 179.

they deal with a highly concrete historical reality: the abdication of the subject. Beckett's *Ecce Homo* is what human beings have become. As though with eyes drained of tears, they stare silently out of his sentences. The spell they cast, which also binds them, is lifted by being reflected in them. However, the minimal promise of happiness they contain, which refuses to be traded for comfort, cannot be had for a price less than total dislocation, to the point of worldlessness." For Adorno, the power of Beckett, as of Franz Kafka, derives from the fact that he works by dismantling appearance, by penetrating the carapace of objectivism, and hence, exploding from within "the art which committed proclamation subjugates from without, and hence only in appearance." He therefore suggests: "He over whom Kafka's wheels have passed, has lost for ever . . . any peace with the world. . . ."[4]

Much the same might be said of Pinter or of Orton. The anarchic nature of the latter's plots, his obsessive concern with incestuous relationships, his delight in absurd situations and improbable coincidences, are all aspects of a subversive attitude. A sense of order and rationality, or causality and recognisable structure, is, of course, prerequisite for the effective exercise of authority. If people refuse to conform to fixed notions of propriety, or to behave rationally, if events generate their own logic, and if language provides little more than an ironic comment on action which defies equally the laws of probability and those of good taste (the laws of taste themselves constituting a declaration of faith in moderation, in law and order, social and metaphysical), then the apparatus of power is effectively thrown out of gear. Orton was that rare phenomenon in English theatre—a genuine anarchist, and like Stoppard and Beckett he turned to farce as his model, though a type of farce thoroughly subverted by anarchy. As one of Sławomir Mrożek's characters remarks in *Tango* (significantly, a play which Stoppard chose to translate), tragedy is perhaps no longer possible, having been displaced by farce. With Orton's treatment, this farce is profoundly subversive—reaching out beyond the figures of authority

[4]Ibid., pp. 190–191.

whom he constantly attacks to sexual identity, social forms and language itself.

Adorno suggests that a bourgeois audience can accommodate itself to almost any ideological material, provided only that the material present itself as a version of realism: "By contrast," he insists, "when the social contract with reality is abandoned, and literary works no longer speak as though they were reporting fact, hairs start to bristle."[5] Though I suspect that this situation has changed—film, television and advertising having domesticated innovation—there is plainly unease in the face of non-realistic modes which hints that some truth remains in this observation. As Adorno suggests, the unintelligible is also capable of provoking a shock, of destabilising. Viewed in this light, the socialist writer—reliant on a rational model, determined that character, historical reality and language expose themselves fully—could be seen as offering reassurance rather than subversion.

But in fact this instability has invaded the work of these socialist writers—not merely a sense of disillusionment, but doubt about the nature and status of art and of simple models of social action. Whereas earlier they had taken their own energetic style—the scrambling together of form and experiences, the irreverence behind their portraits of those in power—as itself constituting something of an antidote to repression, now it begins to seem, paradoxically, that this style may have served simply to underpin repression. As Adorno objects of Brecht's *Arturo Ui*, the risk is that "The true horror of fascism is conjured away, . . ."; or, as he says of Charlie Chaplin's *The Great Dictator*, in which a Jewish girl strikes a line of storm-troopers on their heads with a frying pan—and with impunity, "For the sake of political commitment, political reality is trivialized . . . ."[6] It is, after all, Adorno who says of Beckett's plays that they "have an effect by comparison with which officially committed works look like pantomimes," for

[5] Ibid., p. 180.
[6] Ibid., pp. 184–185.

they "arouse the fear which existentialism merely talks about."[7]

Some such conviction, I take it, led Edgar and Hare in the direction which they seem to have taken. Apparently, they have come to feel that the nexus which potentially yields up the full meaning of experience is not merely between private and public, but between subjective and objective perception. The self-doubt which has entered their work, their doubts about language (expressed most directly by Caryl Churchill in *Traps* [1977]), may threaten the hard-edged reality of their social models, but it also subverts, inevitably, the notion of authority itself. In *Licking Hitler,* Hare attacks what he regards as the corrosive national habit of lying, but he does so with the lies of art and in a play where the real is problematic on a number of levels. It is true that he is concerned with the level at which individuals and societies remain trapped in their experiences and their myths, but the route out of these experiences and these myths remains unclear—the more so when one realises that language may be corrupting and is corruptible, that it not only is an agent of power but also shapes the way we perceive power in the first place.

Edgar shares some of Hare's assumptions and even something of his judgement on the fate of socialist theatre. Nonetheless, he remains clear, at least in his public pronouncements, about the necessity for a socialist future. But his imagination is always transcending societal questions, his work acknowledging elements of self-doubt which make him apprehensive that his commitments may be misunderstood. This ambiguity is apparent in *Mary Barnes* (1978). Set in a community mental home, this drama makes predictable points about the social origins and definitions of insanity, the actual moral schizophrenia of society, and the nature and apparatus of authority. But it does so in a context where that metaphor is extended beyond the perimeter of the purely social. The reconstruction of a personality is presented as an

[7]Ibid., p. 191.

analogue to the reconstruction of society, but it also poses a metaphysical question: how can selfhood be sustained when it is under assault from without and within? The simplifications offered by the characters are themselves available for judgement. Both Edgar and his audience feel the inadequacy of the social metaphor, the distrust of authority extending to the writer himself (as it does not, for example, to a writer like Gooch). The stuttering end of the play constitutes a deliberate refusal of completion—a resistance even to the patterns elaborated by Edgar's own characters.

Much the same could be said of *The Jail Diary of Albie Sachs,* where identity is once again placed under extreme stress—this time, it is quite manifest, socially imposed—as a white lawyer is imprisoned by the South African government. But the imprisonment is never presented as a purely social fact. Indeed, Edgar resists the possibility of caricaturing the South African authorities, and even the temptation to offer a detailed analysis of the political situation. His concern lies elsewhere, in part at least in the aesthetic problems of the writer. He has Albie contemplate the best way of communicating his experience: "At first it was a book. But books are flat, controlled. The stuff of life is rolled up flat and sliced in two-dimensional pages. I wanted something more immediate, more active, more alive. So it had to be a play. And working on the play is fighting back. The worse the things they do, the more I suffer, the better, richer, deeper is the play."[8] The play which Albie envisages is pseudo-Brechtian, the individual sufferings of the prisoners being fused into a communal experience by singing. Apart from anything else, this is a fair description of much English socialist theatre, which sees itself as live and vital evidence of rebellion and incorporates songs designed to play just such a role. But Albie is also tempted by a more metaphysical drama, in which "the playwright writes his play within the play."[9] He comes to feel, however, that "the real problem is to show just what it's like, in isolation, the disintegration, and the horror of it all, to people who are not

[8]David Edgar, *The Jail Diary of Albie Sachs* (London, 1978), p. 43.
[9]Ibid., p. 44.

alone, because they are together, watching, as an audience, my play." As a means to this end he offers three minutes of silence during which there is virtually no action and the individual members of the audience are driven back upon themselves, into the inner world which has also been Albie's only resource. And yet, of course, the irony is that he is creating a play within a play, and hence the metaphysical dimension is allowed to add perspective to the drama.

Edgar recognises a truth frequently resisted by left-wing writers—namely that, whatever the causes, we suffer individually. It may be as a class or as a race that we are persecuted, but it is as individuals that we feel the immediate effects of that persecution. Indeed, it is that very isolation which creates the need for others. Yet that process is inherently ambiguous, for the same impulse which may pull the individual towards Marx may also pull him towards God. The qualities necessary for survival may prove the very qualities which have to be abandoned if the battle is to be won. *The Jail Diary of Albie Sachs* ends ambiguously. In an important respect, it is the story of a defeated man. But the real subtlety of the play lies in the conception that the origins of the defeat go deeper than a failure to analyse the situation correctly; they go deeper than Albie Sachs can himself penetrate, beyond the language which he can command. The battle for South Africa, conceded in the final lines to be essentially a matter for Blacks, is not, in an important respect, the primary subject of the play. *The Jail Diary of Albie Sachs,* like the work of Hare and Poliakoff and even (despite his public pronouncements) Bond, begins to explore not just the lines of force which connect private and public experience, but the uncertain language which is the imperfect tool of that exploration; and it begins to explore as well the nature of the real, which these playwrights had once assumed so self-evident, but which now seems problematic.

The unease which lay beneath the surface of much fifties drama now invades contemporary socialist theatre in England, and to some degree the distinction between these plays and the work of Pinter, Beckett, or even (despite the political differences) Stoppard, begins to blur. The insecurity and alienation which this drama now explores can no longer be wished away with a simple transformation of the political system. It is rooted not simply in a sense of national crisis but in a sense of cultural alarm at the collapse of formal structures of meaning.

Chronology of Important Dates:
First Performances in London Theatres

1955	Samuel Beckett	*Waiting for Godot*	Arts
1956	John Osborne	*Look Back in Anger*	Royal Court
1957	Robert Bolt	*Flowering Cherry*	Haymarket
1958	Ann Jellicoe	*The Sport of My Mad Mother*	Royal Court
	Harold Pinter	*The Birthday Party*	Lyric
	Shelagh Delaney	*A Taste of Honey*	Royal
	Peter Shaffer	*Five Finger Exercise*	Comedy
	Arnold Wesker	*Chicken Soup with Barley*	Royal Court
1959	John Arden	*Serjeant Musgrave's Dance*	Royal Court
	N. F. Simpson	*One Way Pendulum*	Royal Court
1960	John Mortimer	*The Wrong Side of the Park*	Cambridge
1961	Henry Livings	*Stop It, Whoever You Are*	Arts
1962	David Rudkin	*Afore Night Come*	Arts
1963	James Saunders	*Next Time I'll Sing to You*	Arts
	Joan Littlewood	*Oh What a Lovely War*	Royal
1965	Charles Wood	*Meals on Wheels*	Royal Court
	Edward Bond	*Saved*	Royal Court
1966	John McGrath	*Events While Guarding the Bofors Gun*	Hampstead
	Christopher Hampton	*When Did You Last See Your Mother?*	Royal Court
1967	Alan Ayckbourn	*Relatively Speaking*	Duke of York's
	Tom Stoppard	*Rosencrantz and Guildenstern Are Dead*	Old Vic
	David Storey	*The Restoration of Arnold Middleton*	Royal Court

	Peter Nichols	*A Day in the Death of Joe Egg*	Comedy
	Brian Friel	*Philadelphia, Here I Come!*	Lyric
1968	Alan Bennett	*Forty Years On*	Apollo
1969	Peter Barnes	*The Ruling Class*	Piccadilly
1970	Michael Frayn	*The Two of Us*	Garrick
1971	David Hare	*Slag*	Royal Court
	Heathcote Williams	*AC/DC*	Royal Court
	Trevor Griffiths	*Occupations*	The Place
1973	Howard Brenton	*Magnificence*	Royal Court
1974	Mustapha Matura	*Play Mas*	Royal Court
1975	Caryl Churchill	*Objections to Sex and Violence*	Royal Court
	Barry Collins	*Judgement*	I.C.A.
	Stephen Poliakoff	*City Sugar*	Bush
	Howard Barker	*Stripwell*	Royal Court
1977	Barrie Keefe	*Gimme Shelter*	Soho Poly
	David Edgar	*Destiny*	Aldwych

Notes on the Editor and Contributors

GUIDO ALMANSI teaches at the University of East Anglia and is author of *The Writer as Liar: Narrative Technique in the Decameron* and an essay on Pinter.

C. W. E. BIGSBY teaches at the University of East Anglia and is author of *Confrontation and Commitment: A Study of Contemporary American Drama, 1959–66, Dada and Surrealism,* and a study of Joe Orton. He was associate editor of *Stratford-upon-Avon Studies, 19: Contemporary English Drama.*

JOHN RUSSELL BROWN teaches dramaturgy at the State University of New York at Stony Brook and is an Associate Director of the National Theatre of Great Britain. He has directed many plays by contemporary writers, including Beckett, Ionesco, Pinter, Handke, and Kroetz. He edited the earlier Twentieth Century Views volume on *Modern British Dramatists* published in 1968.

GARETH LLOYD EVANS teaches in the Extramural Department of the University of Birmingham. He is author of *J. B. Priestley: The Dramatist* and of a series of books on Shakespeare's life and works; he is also a drama critic for the *Guardian.*

JULIAN HILTON teaches at the University of East Anglia and has studied and taught in Germany. His study of Georg Büchner was published in 1982.

CHRISTOPHER INNES teaches at York University, Toronto, and is author of books on German theatre and of *Holy Theatre: Ritual and the Avant Garde.*

WALTER KERR has been drama critic for the *New York Times* for many years and has written numerous books on plays and playwriting.

COLIN LUDLOW has written a series of theatre reviews for *London Magazine.*

BENEDICT NIGHTINGALE is drama reviewer for the *New Statesman* and author of *An Introduction to 50 Modern British Plays.*

JUNE SCHLUETER teaches at Lafayette College and is author of *Metafictional Characters in Modern Drama* (1979).

KATHARINE J. WORTH is Head of the Department of Drama at Royal Holloway College, London, and author of books on twentieth-century English, Irish, and French playwrights.

HERSH ZEIFMAN teaches at York University, Toronto, and has published articles on Beckett and other modern playwrights. He is book review editor of *Modern Drama*.

Selected Bibliography:
Books on Modern British Theatre

Bigsby, C. W. E., ed. *Stratford-upon-Avon Studies, 19: Contemporary English Drama*. London: Edward Arnold 1981. A collection of especially commissioned essays, including studies of Orton, Osborne and Stoppard, together with accounts of several dramatists who gained attention first in the 1970s.

Brown, John Russell. *Theatre Language: A Study of Arden, Osborne, Pinter, and Wesker*. London: Allen Lane, 1972. An analytical study of theatrical techniques.

Brown, John Russell, ed. *Modern British Dramatists: A Collection of Critical Essays*. Englewood Cliffs, N.J.: Prentice-Hall, 1968. An anthology that covers the period 1955 to 1965; the predecessor of the present volume. Robert Brustein, Martin Esslin, Charles Marowitz, and Raymond Williams are among the critics contributing.

Evans, Gareth Lloyd. *The Language of Modern Drama*. London: Dent, 1977. An independent and clear-sighted appraisal of contemporary drama within its literary and theatrical traditions.

Itzin, Catherine. *Stages in the Revolution: Political Theatre in Britain since 1968*. London: Eyre Methuen, 1980. A valuable collection of manifestoes and self-appraisals by numerous dramatists.

Nightingale, Benedict. *An Introduction to 50 Modern British Plays*. London: Pan Books, 1982. A far more scholarly and thorough study than its title suggests. Thirteen of the writers who are "introduced" through their plays belong to the post–Second World War period.

Taylor, John Russell. *Anger and After: A Guide to the New British Drama*. London: Methuen, 1962; revised ed., 1969. Subsequently published as *The Angry Theatre*. (New York: Hill and Wang, 1962. The most comprehensive account of the dramatists who started writing in the 1950s; plot outlines of many plays are provided together with a description of theatrical conditions in Britain at this time.

Taylor, John Russell. *The Second Wave.* London: Methuen, 1971. A sequel to *Anger and After,* taking the narrative up to 1970.

Worth, Katharine J. *Revolutions in Modern English Drama.* London: G. Bell, 1972. A study that relates recent drama to the earlier experiments of Shaw, Joyce, Auden, Eliot, Coward, and O'Casey.

Books on Individual Dramatists

JOHN ARDEN

Arden, John. *To Present the Pretence: Essays on the Theatre and Its Public.* London: Eyre Methuen, 1977. A self-appraisal as well as a challenging account of contemporary theatre, written when the dramatist had turned away from the direction of his early writings.

Hunt, Albert. *Arden: A Study of His Plays.* London: Eyre Methuen, 1974. A thorough, rather than a critical, assessment.

ALAN AYCKBOURN

Watson, Ian. *Conversations with Ayckbourn.* London: Macdonald Futura, 1981. The best introduction to this dramatist and one that alerts a reader to his distinctive humour.

EDWARD BOND

Coult, Tony. *The Plays of Edward Bond.* London: Eyre Methuen, 1977. An engaging introduction that considers a number of recurring themes and describes the variety of the dramatist's theatrical style.

Hay, Malcolm, and Roberts, Philip. *Bond: A Study of His Plays.* London: Eyre Methuen, 1980. A careful account of the dramatist's career enlivened by long quotations from letters, notes, and other documentation.

JOE ORTON

Lahr, John. *Prick up Your Ears: The Biography of Joe Orton.* London: Allen Lane, 1978. A critical assessment as well as a biography.

JOHN OSBORNE

Banham, Martin. *Osborne.* Edinburgh: Oliver and Boyd, 1969. The best of a number of short books on the career of this dramatist who has promised to tell the story himself in a second volume of his autobiography.

HAROLD PINTER

Esslin, Martin. *The Peopled Wound.* London: Methuen, New York: Doubleday, 1970. A pursuit of the meaning and significance of the plays.

Ganz, Arthur, ed. *Pinter: A Collection of Critical Essays.* Englewood Cliffs, N.J.: Prentice-Hall, 1972. An anthology of criticism.

Quigley, Austin E. *The Pinter Problem.* Princeton, N.J.: Princeton University Press, 1975. Valuable for clear accounts of the structure and action of the plays.

ARNOLD WESKER

Leeming, Glenda, and Trussler, Simon. *The Plays of Arnold Wesker: An Assessment.* London: Victor Gollancz, 1971. An account and defense of the dramatist's development.

Index